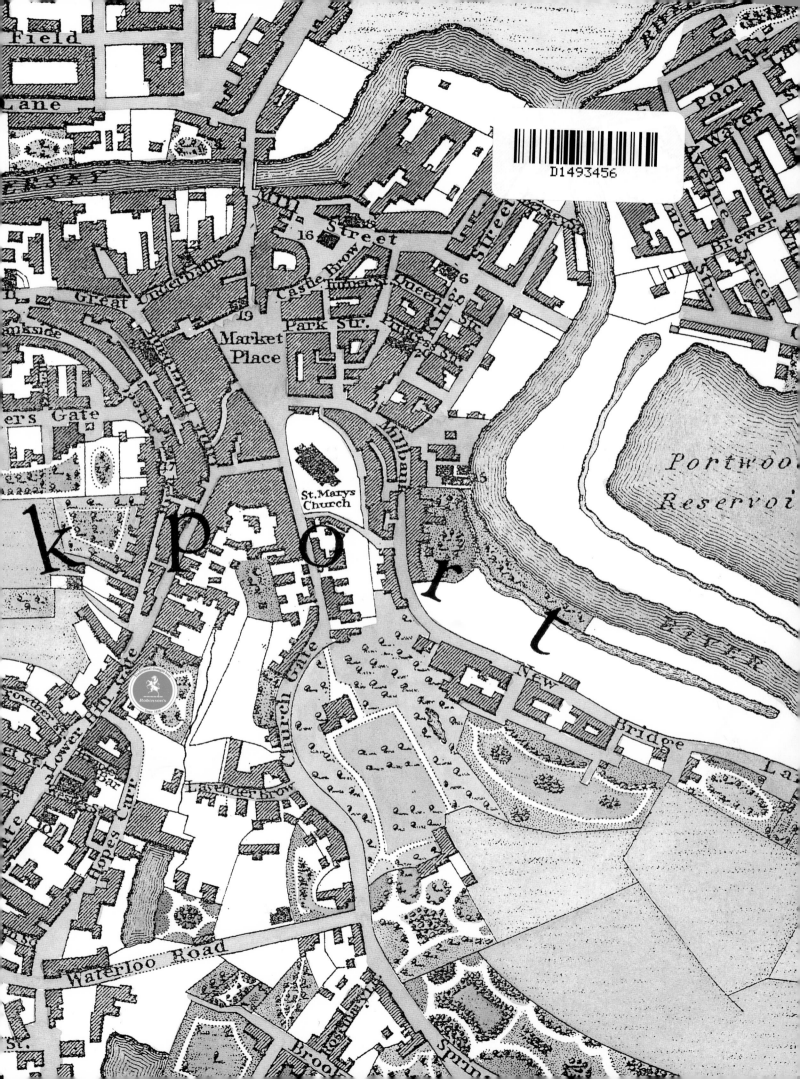

"Stockport boasts its springs and fountains, Many streets as steep as mountains,
Rosy cheeks and bright-eyed lasses, Youths which toast them in their glasses,
Church and castle, tower and steeple, And a loyal, happy people."

Barnaby's Journal

'A Toast'

*During a Robinson's staff dinner in 1952,
at Lyme Hall, Disley, Mr A Radcliffe,
who had served the company for 52 years,
stood up and proposed this toast:*

"The House of Robinson"

*"Let us pay tribute to those who toiled
with grit and determination and held the
fort in the past; to those who valiantly
hold the fort and keep the flag flying
today; and to those reinforcements round
the corner who will be called upon to
guide our destiny in the future.
For years the house of Robinson has
been controlled by gentlemen endowed
with wisdom to comprehend; judgement
to define; courteous in manner and
steady and firm in principle.
Loyalty and service will continue to
merit the confidence and esteem of the
Directors. Let us hand down to those
who come after us, a legacy of efficiency."*

DEDICATION

This book is dedicated to the memory
of Lady Robinson, wife of Sir John Robinson, who was
so looking forward to reading it after contributing so much,
but, unfortunately, died aged 92, just before publication.
Her sons, Peter, Dennis and David, acknowledge their and
the Company's immense debt to her
for ensuring the continuity of the family business
and the Robinson brewing tradition.

THE HISTORY OF ROBINSON'S BREWERY

Dr Lynn F. Pearson

Published in Great Britain in 1997 by Morris Nicholson Cartwright Limited,
161-163 Ashley Road, Hale, Altrincham, Cheshire WA15 9SD.

British Library Cataloguing-in-Publication Data
A catalogue record for this book is available from the British Library.

ISBN 0 9529461 0 6

Designed and produced by Morris Nicholson Cartwright Ltd.

Photoset by Bye-word, Manchester.

Originated in Great Britain by Qualitech Photo Litho, Stockport.
Printed by The Cavendish Press, Leicester. Bound by Hunter & Foulis Ltd, Edinburgh.

ACKNOWLEDGEMENTS

The author would like to record her thanks to the Robinson family
for their kind co-operation during the compilation of this history.

The publishers especially thank Mark Sheppard and Elie Barakat for their invaluable research.

BIBLIOGRAPHY

BUSINESS ARCHIVES *Records of Frederic Robinson Limited, Stockport.*
PARLIAMENTARY PAPERS *HC 1892 (294-1) LXVIII, On-licenses return.*

NEWSPAPERS, DIRECTORIES AND RELATED LOCAL MATERIAL
Manpower Services, Unicorn Brewery, Stockport, Site Survey *(1983)*
Municipal School of Technology, Manchester, Calendar for the Session 1911-12 *(1911)*
Stalybridge Reporter · Stockport Advertiser
Directories of Stockport, Cheshire and Lancashire from 1834
Maps and other material from local studies sections of Stockport and Stalybridge libraries.

BOOKS
Ashmore, Owen, The Industrial Archaeology of Stockport
(Department of Extra Mural Studies, University of Manchester 1975)
Barber, Norman, Where have all the breweries gone? *(CAMRA/Richardson 1982)*
Hawkins, K H and Pass, C L, The Brewing Industry *(Heinemann 1979)*
Jacobson, Michael, 200 Years of Beer – The Story of Boddingtons' Strangeways Brewery 1778-1978
(Boddingtons' Breweries Ltd 1978)
Ogden, Mike A History of Stockport Breweries *(Richardson 1987)*
Owen, Colin C 'The Greatest Brewery in the World' - A History of Bass, Ratcliff & Gretton
(Derbyshire Record Society 1992)
Richmond, Lesley and Turton, Alison (eds), The Brewing Industry, A Guide to Historical Records
(Manchester University Press 1990)
Walton, John K, Lancashire, A Social History 1558 - 1939 *(Manchester University Press 1987)*

ARTICLES
Wilson, Richard, The British Brewing Industry since 1750, in Richmond and Turton, op cit

PHOTOGRAPHIC ACKNOWLEDGEMENTS

Roy Westall · Manchester Public Library · Stockport Public Library
Stalybridge Public Library · Marple Local History Society · Chester Record Office
'Local Brew' by B. Sullivan

PUBLISHING

CONTENTS

Frederic Robinson Ltd, Unicorn Brewery, Stockport.

FOREWORD

THE STORY of the Robinson's brewery is one that we are very proud to be part of. This history is a salute to the five generations of the Robinson family who were the custodians of our business before us – and an introduction for the generations to follow us.

From the opening of the first of our houses over 150 years ago, to the present day, the constant theme of the Robinson family has been that of traditional standards and values, but always with quality first.

Throughout the development of our fine ales and investment in production, to the expansion of our estate, the commitment to our customers' comfort and enjoyment has never been less than total.

We will never be old-fashioned, but we will never let our old-fashioned values slip. It is our tradition, and we guard it jealously.

Peter, Dennis and David Robinson

*The Legh Arms dates from the early 15th Century and is situated in Prestbury Village.
At the time of the 1745 rebellion under the name of the Black Boy, the Inn accommodated
Bonnie Prince Charlie on his way south.*

PREFACE

Frederic Robinson was an entrepreneur, a brewer and a family man. Soon after 1859, when he took over the inn which his father and brother had run before him, Frederic began to expand the brewing business which eventually became Frederic Robinson Limited.

Quality ales were always a Robinson's hallmark, and it was this commitment to customers which helped the company survive the vicissitudes of the brewery wars around the turn of the century. Family involvement was vital, of course. When Robinson's became a limited company in 1920, it was Frederic's wife Emma who was the driving force behind that decision; she had been prominent in Robinson's affairs for six decades, giving essential stability in changing times.

Robinson's, now a leading regional brewer, has survived in the highly competitive world of modern brewing by combining forward thinking with an adherence to the best traditions. Out at Bredbury, the Unicorn Packaging Centre handles an astonishing number of bottles and kegs per hour, while in Stockport the Unicorn Brewery still counts draught ales amongst its products and the award-winning shire horse team continues its deliveries.

This engaging story of a family business is also a microcosm of the history of the British brewing industry. I am sure that Frederic Robinson, who endeavoured to brew the finest ales in the 1860s, would have been proud of the company he created as it now looks towards the next century of brewing.

Dr Lynn F. Pearson.

THE ORIGIN OF THE UNICORN

Sᴛᴏᴄᴋᴘᴏʀᴛ ᴀᴛ the start of the 1820's was a town which had changed radically within a generation, transformed by the rise of the cotton industry from a small market town, with less than 5,000 inhabitants, in the early 1770's to a mill town of over 21,000 by 1821. Meadows and an orchard formed the setting when the Unicorn Inn was built on Lower Hillgate in 1722, but by 1827, when the Robinson story begins, the inn was part of Stockport's urban centre.

Lᴏᴡᴇʀ ʜɪʟʟɢᴀᴛᴇ leads upwards and southwards out of Stockport along the valley of the Tin (or Carr) Brook, a small stream which eventually flows into the Mersey. The Unicorn Inn was built on the east side of the street by John Warner, who later leased out part of the land at the rear, backing on to the stream, to Samuel Lees. There Lees erected a water-powered calendar house; a calendar is a press, in the form of rollers, used for finishing linen cloth. By 1731 a brewhouse, owned by John Warren, was recorded on the Unicorn site.

An explanation of how the famous Unicorn emblem came about is in this extract from a series in the Stockport Advertiser 1888, entitled 'Recollections of Stockport'

"Sixty years ago this old hostelry had, for its hostess, Mrs Sarah Patterson, a widow. In our museum may be seen a large jug which once did service at the Unicorn, on which is inscribed the name of Mrs Patterson. Other relics of bygone days may still be seen in this old inn. The present hostess if required, will show her visitors a horn, which is said once adorned the head of that mythological and certainly extinct, animal, the Unicorn."

Stockport Market Place 1859, the year Frederic commenced brewing.

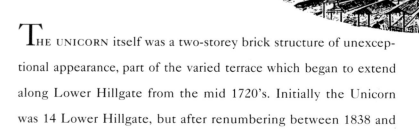

Tʜᴇ ᴜɴɪᴄᴏʀɴ itself was a two-storey brick structure of unexceptional appearance, part of the varied terrace which began to extend along Lower Hillgate from the mid 1720's. Initially the Unicorn was 14 Lower Hillgate, but after renumbering between 1838 and

Lower Hillgate c.1910.

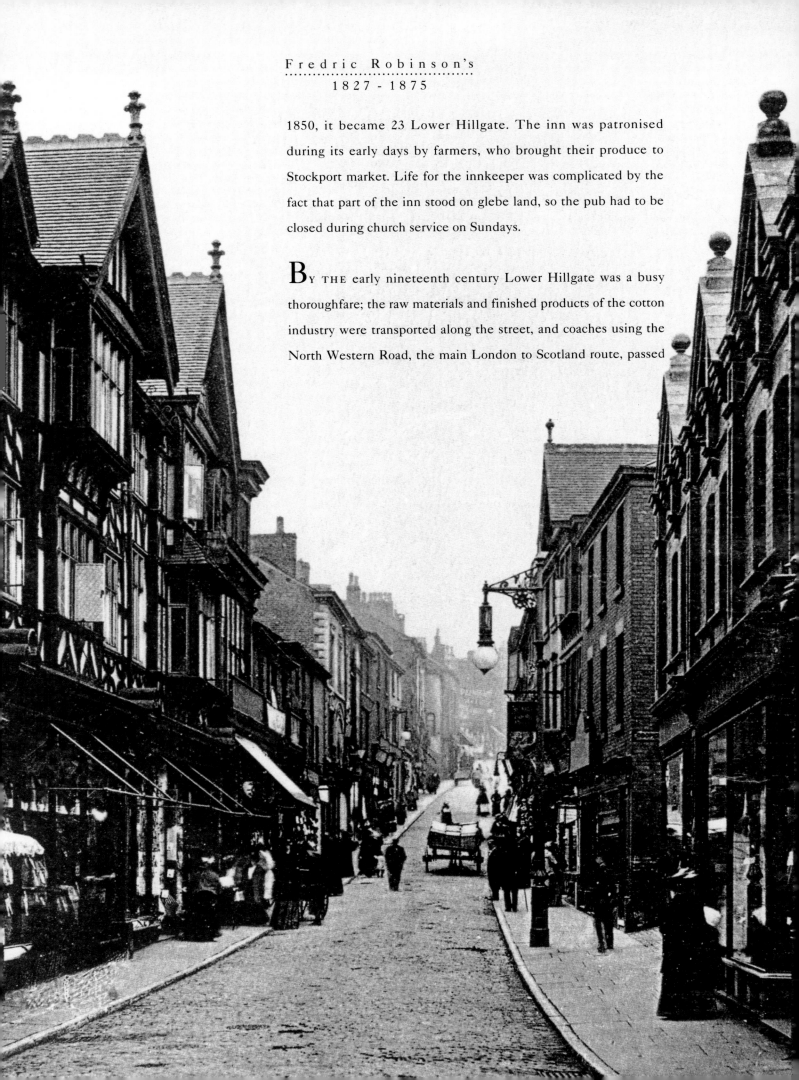

1850, it became 23 Lower Hillgate. The inn was patronised during its early days by farmers, who brought their produce to Stockport market. Life for the innkeeper was complicated by the fact that part of the inn stood on glebe land, so the pub had to be closed during church service on Sundays.

By THE early nineteenth century Lower Hillgate was a busy thoroughfare; the raw materials and finished products of the cotton industry were transported along the street, and coaches using the North Western Road, the main London to Scotland route, passed close by. The Unicorn was occupied by several innkeepers in quick succession during this period: Henry Hicton in 1809, John Wright around 1814-16, Ralph Morton in 1823 and widow Mrs Sarah Patterson in 1824-6. The following year marked the start of the Robinson family association with the Unicorn, when William Robinson became landlord in 1826.

WILLIAM ROBINSON was born at Northenden, near Sale, in 1800. He married Juliet Shaw at Northenden on the 4th February 1822 and they moved to Prestbury, near Macclesfield. Their first child, George, was born in 1825 and the second, Mary, followed in 1826. William worked as a cotton-overlooker at nearby Bollington, a small, stone-built cotton town nestling in the Pennine foothills. We do not know why William chose to leave the cotton trade and move to Stockport, but perhaps the combination of a growing family, and unrest amongst the local textile workers, suggested that innkeeping was a better financial proposition.

STOCKPORT WAS one of the earliest northern textile areas to become trade unionised – the mule spinners organised in 1792 – and many workers later became involved with radical political reform movements. This activity reached its height at a mass meeting in Manchester on the 16th August 1819, when Stockport's representatives were at the forefront of events leading to what has become known as the Peterloo Massacre. Lancashire weavers rioted during the 1826 depression, so perhaps it is no surprise that William Robinson was keen to move out of the textile trade.

AROUND THE time of their arrival at the Unicorn, the Robinsons had a second son, William, who died when aged only one month. This not uncommon tragedy was the first in a series of four infant deaths; a second William, born in 1828, James, born 1830, and a third William, born 1832, all failed to survive beyond three years. It was 1834 before Juliet produced another child who survived into

THE UNICORN INN	
23 Lower Hillgate, Stockport	
PAST INNKEEPERS	
1809 - 1814*	Henry Hicton
1814 - 1816*	John Wright
1820 - 1824	Ralph Morton
1824 - 1826	Sarah Patterson
1826 - 1850	William Robinson
1850 - 1865	George Robinson
1865 - 1883	Frederic Robinson
1883 - 1886	Abraham Baxter
1886 - 1890	Martha Baxter
1890 - 1892	John Grundy
1892 - 1898	George Eastwood
1898 - 1899	William McMurray
1899 - 1902	Hiriam Anderson
1902 - 1904	James Hopkins
1904 - 1911	John Oulton
1911 - 1912	Annie Woodhead
1912 - 1915	John Harry Thompson
1915 - 1916	John Leach Doughty
1916 - 1917	Henry Simpson
1917 - 1928	Frank Hallworth
1928 -	Alfred Parkinson
1928 - 1930	Thomas Nixon
1930 - 1934	John Jarvis
1934 - 1935	Ida Eyre
*Approximate dates	
7th March 1935	Renewal refused
29th March 1935	Renewal referred to Compensation Authority
24th Dec. 1935	Compensation Money paid
31st Dec. 1935	House closed

Past innkeepers at the Unicorn Inn on Lower Hillgate up till its closure on the 31st December 1935.

The Manchester Yeoman Cavalry dispersing the crowd at the Peterloo Massacre – painting by George Cruikshank.

Ordinance Survey from 1895 showing the Unicorn Inn on Lower Hillgate.

(Right) The start of the Robinson Family association with the Unicorn, when William Robinson became Landlord in 1826.

County of Chester.

(Dodge, Printer, Stockport.)

At A GENERAL MEETING of his Majesty's Justices of the Peace, acting in and for the Division of STOCKPORT, in the Hundred of MACCLESFIELD, in the County aforesaid, held at the DOG and PARTRIDGE INN, STOCKPORT, in the Division and County aforesaid, on Thursday the Seventh day of September, One Thousand Eight Hundred and Twenty Six.

William Robinson — at the Sign of the Unicorn, in the Township of Stockport — Victualler, acknowledges himself to be indebted to our Sovereign Lord the King, in the sum of Thirty Pounds, and James Booth — of Stockport aforesaid Cordwainer, acknowledges himself to be indebted to our Sovereign Lord the King in the sum of Twenty Pounds, to be levied upon their several goods and chattels, lands and tenements, by way of recognizance, to his Majesty's use, his heirs and successors, upon condition that the said William Robinson do and shall keep the true assize in uttering and selling Bread and Victuals, Beer, Ale, and other Liquors, in his, her, or their house, and shall not fraudulently dilute or adulterate the same, and shall not use in uttering and selling thereof, any pots or other measures that are not full size, and shall not wilfully or knowingly permit drunkenness or tippling, nor get drunk in his, her, or their house or other premises, nor knowingly suffer any gaming with cards, draughts, dice, bagatelle, or any other sendentary game, in his, her, or their house, or any of the out-houses, appurtenances, or easements thereunto belonging, by Journeymen, Labourers, Servants, or Apprentices; nor knowingly introduce, permit, or suffer any Bull, Bear, or Badger baiting, Cock fighting or other such sport or amusement in any part of his, her, or their premises, nor shall knowingly, or designedly, and with a view to harbour and entertain such, permit or suffer men or women of notoriously bad fame, or dissolute girls and boys, to assemble and meet together in his, her or their house, or any of the premises thereto belonging; nor shall keep open his, her or their house, nor permit or suffer any drinking, or tippling, in any part of his, her, or their premises, during the usual hours of Divine Service on Sundays, nor shall keep open his, her, or their house or other premises, during late hours of the night, or early in the morning, for any other purpose then the reception of Travellers, but do keep good rule and order therein according to the purport of a licence granted for selling Ale, Beer, or other Liquors, by retail in the said house and premises, for one whole year, commencing on the Tenth day of October next, than this recognizance to be void or else to remain in full force.

Taken and acknowledged before us

adulthood, Jane, followed by Frederic in 1836. Despite these difficulties, William and Juliet made a great success of running the Unicorn, and were able to buy the inn from Samuel Hole on the 29th September 1838.

WILLIAM ROBINSON chose not to brew his own beer and traded solely as a retailer, perhaps because of his lack of brewing experience. Also, beer was readily available from the various Stockport breweries and possibly from the three other inns on Lower Hillgate; the Plough, the Bishop Blaize and the Spread Eagle, which all produced home brewed ales. The Plough's brewhouse may only have functioned from the 1830s, while the Bishop Blaize brewhouse only seems to have produced enough ale for the pub itself. Brewing at the Spread Eagle's Eagle Brewery, which probably supplied at least two pubs, had begun well before William took over the Unicorn. It is likely that the Spread Eagle, or one of Stockport's larger breweries, was the source of the Unicorn's ale. The Spread Eagle itself was eventually to become part of the Robinson estate.

For over ten years William and Juliet continued their retail business at the Unicorn, and Juliet bore two more daughters, Harriet in 1839 and Juliet in 1841, who both died at the age of five years. Soon after baby Juliet's death, William's wife died, and by 1849 he had left the inn; he moved to Heaton Norris and married again, to Harriet, about whom nothing more is known. The Unicorn was left in the hands of his elder son George, by then married to Clarissa Chadwick from Cheadle; their daughter, Harriet Juliet, was born in 1849. William's younger son Frederic, then aged thirteen, had left the Inn to live with his sister Jane, a dressmaker. George and Clarissa ran the Unicorn with the help of Clarissa's sister Sarah Ann, and perhaps as a result of George's childhood experience at the inn, began to brew their own ale on the premises - the first Robinson ale.

The couple stayed at the Unicorn for ten years, leaving in the summer of 1859, when Frederic returned to become landlord. At this time, the licensed trade in Stockport was highly competitive. Apart from the Unicorn, there were at least twenty-two other licensed outlets on Hillgate alone. By 1865, the Unicorn was only one amongst the 163 inns and taverns of Stockport, not forgetting the 121 beerhouses. All five breweries in close proximity to the Unicorn were anxious to sell their wares to innkeepers who currently brewed their own beer.

THE UNICORN INN 23 Lower Hillgate, Stockport		
1841 CENSUS RETURNS		
William Robinson	(40)	*Publican*
Julia Robinson	(40)	*Wife*
Mary Robinson	(15)	*Daughter*
George Robinson	(15)	*Son*
Jane Robinson	(7)	*Daughter*
Frederic Robinson	(5)	*Son*
Harriet Robinson	(3)	*Daughter*
Juliet Robinson	(3m)	*Daughter*

THE UNICORN INN 23 Lower Hillgate, Stockport		
1851 CENSUS RETURNS		
George Robinson	(25)	*Publican*
Clarissa Robinson	(25)	*Wife*
Harriet Robinson	(1)	*Daughter*
Sarah A Chadwick	(18)	*Barmaid/ Servant*
William Robinson (Moved to High Grove Farm, Heald Green)	(50)	*Farmer of 41 Acres*
Mary Robinson	(25)	*Daughter*

THE UNICORN YARD/UNICORN INN 23 Lower Hillgate, Stockport		
1861 CENSUS RETURNS		
THE UNICORN YARD		
Frederic Robinson	(25)	*Brewer*
THE UNICORN INN		
George Robinson	(36)	*Publican*
Clarissa Robinson	(36)	*Daughter*
Harriet Juliet	(12)	*Scholar*
Thomas William	(6)	*Scholar*
Harry Chadwick	(4)	
Fred	(1)	

The Government census's carried out between 1841-61 project an interesting statistical picture of the Robinson family and their employees. They show clearly each individual resident, their age and occupation.

(Right) Frederic and Emma Robinson (1836 - 1890 and 1839 - 1921).

Frederic and Emma with their son William, and daughter Mary. William, pictured here with his mother, went on to marry Priscilla Needham in 1899, and became Chairman of Frederic Robinson Limited in 1920.

On taking over the Unicorn, Frederic Robinson had to choose between continuing to brew in a small way, stopping brewing completely to become a retailer (as his father had been), or expanding his brewing activities and becoming a wholesaler. He chose the latter course, perhaps attracted by the near-continuous rise in per capita beer consumption which took place during his lifetime. By 1859, an average of twenty-two gallons of beer per person was being drunk every year; almost half a pint a day for every man, woman and child. In the urban areas, wages were rising faster than prices, but there were still few opportunities for recreation outside the public house; competition in the brewing trade was intense, but rewards could be great.

Frederic and Emma with their children (from left) Emma, Eleanor, Mary and William.

FREDERIC'S FIRST step in expanding the brewing operation at the Unicorn was to buy a former warehouse at the back of the inn, and adapt it for brewing. He then began to sell his ales to a wider market than just the Unicorn's customers, and during the 1860s Robinson's became available at many pubs and beerhouses in and around Stockport. His first customer was Mrs Lamb of the Bridge Inn, Chestergate. Expansion also brought problems; most imme-

A horse-drawn low slung dray of the same type as used by Frederic in the early 1870s.

diately, finding an efficient means of delivering the goods. At first Frederic relied on carriers and the railway network to transport his ales locally, but as trade increased, the need for a more reliable and flexible method of delivery became apparent. Horse

An outing from The Bridge Inn, Chestergate, c.1914. Mrs Lamb of The Bridge Inn was Federic's first customer in 1865.

drawn drays (low-slung, flat-bedded carts) were the answer, and the brewing business was profitable enough by the early 1870s for a small fleet to be bought.

FREDERIC'S FAMILY expanded as rapidly as did the brewery in the 1860s. He married Emma Woolley, three years his junior, and between 1862 and 1875 they had ten children; Emma was the first-born followed by William in 1864. Four later children died in infancy, and their only other surviving son was Herbert, born in 1872. Young Emma was eventually to marry Alfred Evan Munton, Robinson's head brewer.

THE END of the beginning of the Robinson story came on Sunday, the 15th August 1875, when William Robinson died at his home in Denby Lane, Heaton Norris, at the age of seventy-eight. He lived long enough to see his investment in the Unicorn bear fruit, as the business expanded from small inn to substantial brewery.

THE MAKING OF A BREWERY

Robinson's first pub was the Railway in Marple Bridge, bought by Frederic in 1876. It has since been rebuilt and re-named The Royal Scot (inset).

THE FINAL quarter of the nineteenth century was a far less propitious time for brewers than the boom years between 1850 and the mid-1870s. Although real wages continued to rise, beer consumption declined and trade competition was intensified by the wide-ranging railway network, which allowed brewers to sell their products on a national scale. In the 1870s Frederic Robinson concentrated on the reliable production of high quality ales, and increased the number of workers at the brewery, which had previously employed only two men.

ALTHOUGH FREDERIC was able to produce fine ales, he had no control over the condition in which beer was sold by independent publicans; the reputation of Robinsons ales could thus be sullied by poor innkeeping. To combat this, Frederic decided to buy a small number of public houses, which became exclusive outlets for Robinsons ales. This guaranteed demand helped the profitability of the brewery, as well as being a showcase for Robinsons.

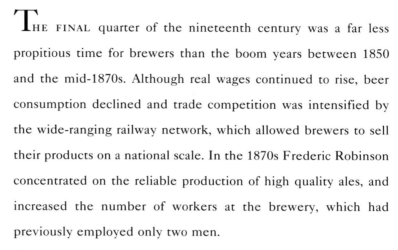

The Peak Forest Canal, Marple Bridge...

THE FIRST pub in the new Robinson's estate was the Railway Inn, in the industrial community of Marple Bridge, about four miles east of Stockport. The houses of Marple Bridge were clustered round a bridge over the River Goyt, just south of Marple locks, a flight of sixteen locks on the Peak Forest Canal. The canal system was used for the transport of beer before the expansion of the railway network; ales from Burton reached Macclesfield via the Macclesfield Canal, which joined the Peak Forest Canal at Marple Bridge. The Railway Inn was close to the village station, (on the Manchester, Sheffield & Lincolnshire Railway), and had competition from the Midland Hotel and the Horse Shoe Inn, as well as several pubs in nearby Marple. The Railway is still a Robinsons house, but was rebuilt in the 1930s and is now known as the Royal Scot.

FREDERIC PURCHASED the Railway on Wednesday, the 3rd May 1876, and the Robinson's name was soon displayed outside the inn; business must have gone well, as he bought a second house, the Wharf Tavern in Ashton-under-Lyne, on the 12th October of the same year. During the remainder of the 1870s and throughout the 1880s Frederic continued buying public houses in Stockport and the surrounding area, in order to build up a secure market for his ales. Other brewers, local and national, were also pursuing the same course, but the quality of Robinson's products ensured a supply of funds sufficient for expansion.

(Above) Old Millgate, c.1890.
On the right is the Arden Arms public
house which still stands today (Top).
A car salesroom now occupies
the site of the thatched cottage.

AMONG THE early Robinson's houses were the Oddfellows Arms in Heaton Norris (rebuilt in 1978 as the Silver Jubilee), the Bush on Stockport Road in Hyde, the Nicholson's Arms on Lancashire Hill in Stockport (rebuilt in 1970 on a nearby site), the Church Inn at Cheadle Hulme, the King's Arms at Fulshaw Cross in Wilmslow, and the Dandy Cock in Disley, which was bought in 1888. All these houses lay in an area to the south-east of Manchester, centred on Stockport, and could be readily supplied from the brewery.

Frederic became the local distributor for
Arthur Guinness & Co. of Dublin.

FREDERIC ALSO undertook expansion of the brewery, overseeing the enlargement of the basic structure and modernisation of the brewing plant to cope with increased demand. In 1876 he began to purchase land and buildings on various sites adjacent to the brewery, a slow process which would eventually provide room for growth. In addition to brewing and selling Robinsons, he became

(Main picture) The Church Inn, Cheadle Hulme c.1910, one of the early pubs acquired by Robinson's in south Manchester in 1880. Little has changed today (above).

the local distributor for Arthur Guinness, Son & Co. of Dublin. The unique Guinness stout did not compete directly with his own ales, and provided a useful extra source of income, particularly since Stockport had a substantial population of Irish descent. Frederic continued to live at the Unicorn, and in 1878 his son William, aged fourteen, became a brewer's assistant. His eldest daughter, Emma, worked at the inn and the four youngest children were still at school; the family were later joined at the inn by Frederic's sister Mary.

By the 1880s Frederic, head of the Robinson family and driving force behind the expansion of the Unicorn Brewery, had become an eminent Stockport citizen. He subscribed to Henry

*Detail of the Register signed by
William and Priscilla.*

Heginbotham's two-volume history Stockport: Ancient and Modern, published in 1882 and 1892, and gave generous financial support to the Little Moor Chapel. On Wednesday, the 2nd October 1889, he and Emma had the pleasure of seeing their elder son William married at St Mary's, Stockport parish church. William, now aged twenty-five, had chosen as his bride Priscilla Needham, the youngest daughter of ironfounder John Needham of Millgate Hall, Stockport. The ceremony took place at 10.30am and was attended by a large gathering, reflecting the keen interest

of the townspeople in the marriage and the union of two of the town's respected families. For her wedding, Priscilla wore a dress of white corded silk, veiled and trimmed with lace, set off by a gold brooch ornamented with pearls and diamonds, which was a gift from William. After the ceremony and the wedding breakfast at Millgate House, the couple left for their honeymoon in North Wales. The brewery employees shared in the festivities, as they were treated to a day's outing to Whaley Bridge, where many toasts were drunk at the White Hart.

The wedding of William and Priscilla took place on Wednesday the 2nd of October 1889, at St. Mary's, Stockport's Parish Church. Priscilla wore a dress of white corded silk, veiled and trimmed with lace, set off by a gold brooch ornamented with pearls and diamonds, which was a gift from William.

27

On Frederic's death in 1890, the Unicorn Brewery passed to his widow
Emma, pictured above at Brook House, Offerton, the family home.

Sadly, only four months after the wedding came the death of Frederic, on the 6th February 1890. The funeral service was held at Little Moor Chapel. He had spent over thirty of his fifty-four years building up the Unicorn Brewery and establishing the Robinson's estate, which by then comprised twelve houses. He took over the Unicorn when it was a small inn and laid the foundations for a substantial brewing business, at a time when competition in the trade was intense. He also improved deliveries, which originally relied upon railway company carriers, by acquiring a horse and dray. The Unicorn Brewery passed to Frederic's widow Emma; their sons William and Herbert both worked at the brewery but William took the larger role in the direction of business matters.

Decorations outside the brewery on Lower Hillgate to celebrate Queen Victoria's Diamond Jubilee. The Town Council voted an expenditure of £750, anxious that locals should enjoy and remember this historic event.

The main problem facing William was still the competition within the trade for secure outlets. Although beer consumption rose again during the 1890s, many breweries found that the only means of acquiring enough capital to continue expanding their estates was to go public, and raise money through the stock market; 234 breweries followed this course between 1886 and 1900. The investing public generally approved of these share issues and pub buying continued apace, making it hard for Robinsons to compete in this market.

In 1892, Robinsons owned only five on-licenses in the Stockport borough licensing district, compared with the three local brewers

DEATH OF A STOCKPORT BREWER

We regret to announce the death of Mr Frederic Robinson of the Unicorn Brewery, Hillgate, Stockport, which took place at his residence, Hall Street, on Thursday evening, at the age of 54 years. The deceased gentleman was seized with illness–internal inflammation – early last Saturday week and Dr Heginbotham J.P. was called in. On the Monday the patient became worse, and Dr Leech, the well-known physician, of Manchester, was called into consultation, and he gave the family little hope of the patient's ultimate recovery. Mr Robinson however gradually got worse until Wednesday forenoon, when there seemed to be an improvement in his condition, and hopes were again held out that he might recover. These proved delusive, and on Thursday morning he became considerably worse and died at a quarter to eleven in the evening. The deceased leaves a widow and grown-up family – two sons and four daughters. The two sons are Mr W Robinson and Mr Herbert Robinson, both of whom are engaged in the business, and will continue the operations of the firm. The father of the deceased a good many years ago had the Unicorn Inn, Lower Hillgate, and brewed for private consumption. About 30 years ago the deceased began as a public brewer, and since that time he has steadily extended his business. Very recently important alterations have been carried out at the brewery, the structure having been considerably enlarged, the brewing plant thoroughly modernised, and the fittings of a first class brewery having been put in so as to enable the firm to cope with their large and increasing trade. It is much to be regretted that the deceased having carried out these alterations should not have lived to see the benefits which must have derived from them. The family attend Little Moor Chapel, of which Mr Robinson was a generous supporter. He was not associated in any way with public affairs, although well qualified to bear his part in the work of the town. He devoted his energies entirely to his own business, and to this no doubt is to be attributed much of the success which has attended his efforts.

The funeral took place on Tuesday at the Stockport Borough Cemetery in the presence of a large number of sympathising friends. The funeral *cortege*, which consisted of a plain hearse and four broughams, left the residence of the deceased shortly after half-past 12 and proceeded to the cemetery by way of Churchgate, Millgate, Underbank and Hillgate. Along the route there was noticeable every mark of esteem for the deceased gentleman, blinds and shutters being drawn on every side.

Stockport Advertiser
14th February 1890.

Henry Bell & Co, Cliftons, and Richard Clarke who owned 25, 17 and 14 respectively. Firms from outside the area were also buying Stockport pubs and beerhouses; thirteen were owned by Thomas Sykes & Co of Burton upon Trent, who took over the local Waterloo Brewery and its licensed estate in 1888. The most significant licensed house owner in Stockport in 1892 was the Brewers Investment Corporation Limited with thirty-five houses. The Corporation was a Birmingham concern formed to make a profit from the sale of freehold and leasehold licensed properties; it bought Marsland's Brookfield Brewery of Stockport, with its licensed estate, in 1889. In the towns and villages around Stockport, Bell & Co was the most significant licensed house owner.

The Unicorn Brewery was enlarged towards the end of 1890, and in the ensuing decade, rather than being tempted to over-invest in licensed property, William Robinson consolidated the position of the brewery and concentrated on the production of fine ales. This decision was later seen to be wise, when per capita beer consumption resumed its decline in the early years of the new century, and breweries with much of their capital tied up in property ran into difficulties.

For the Robinson family, 1891 saw a further extension of the Robinson-Needham union, with the marriage of Frederic's third daughter Eleanor to John Needham. William and Priscilla's first child, Frederic, was also born in the same year. Frederic was the first member of the fourth generation of brewing Robinsons. In 1893 Emma, William's eldest sister, married Robinson's head brewer Alfred Munton, who joined the firm following the 1890 brewery enlargement. William and Priscilla had three further children: John Edgar, born 1895, Priscilla Mabel Juliet, born 1896, and William Cecil, born in 1900, taking Robinson's and the Unicorn into the twentieth century.

The Old Tom Cat has appeared on labels in many different guises since Alfred Munton's first sketch in 1899 (opposite).

The distinctive moulded bottles used by Robinson's around 1920.

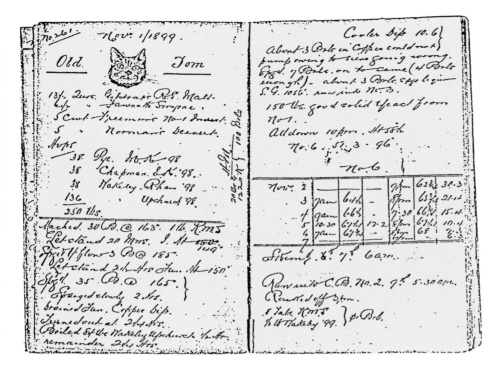

Alfred Munton's notebook open at a page giving details of an Old Tom brew, made on Wednesday 1st November, 1899. It is interesting to compare and contrast Mr Munton's account of this brew with our present picture.

BREWING OLD TOM ALE IN 1899

One of the most precious historical documents possessed by our Company is the personal brewing notebook of Mr Alfred E Munton for 1899. This gentleman was Head Brewer at Unicorn Brewery in the latter years of the nineteenth century and until his death in 1918. He married a Miss Robinson, the daughter of the original Frederic Robinson, from whom the Company takes its name, and was thus great-uncle by marriage to the present Directors.

Mr Munton was a highly skilled brewer who took the keenest interest in every aspect of his craft. He purchased the Company's first microscope for the examination of his yeast and beers, and operated a 'forcing tray' – an early type of incubator – which enabled him to test the keeping qualities of his beers. These pioneering methods of brewing quality control were, of course, to be greatly extended and elaborated by Mr Munton's nephew, another Frederic Robinson, who established our Laboratory in 1911 when he graduated from University, and was later to succeed his uncle as Head Brewer.

Mr Munton made meticulous notes and records of his brewing recipes, materials and methods, and his brewing notebook is packed with these details of each brew. Inevitably he used 'brewer's jargon' and many abbreviations in his notes, which need informed interpretation if the modern reader is to understand the total picture.

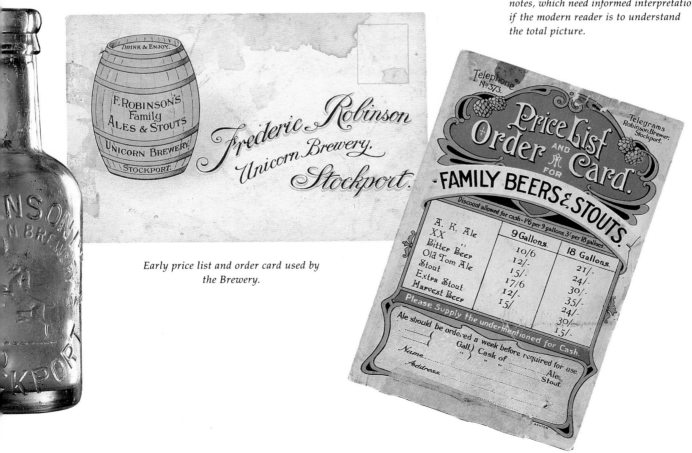

Early price list and order card used by the Brewery.

*A selection of labels, drip mats and general advertising material used
by Robinson's over the years.*

THE UNICORN'S
FIRST ACQUISITION

For the brewing industry in general, times were hard in the first decade of the twentieth century. Not only did beer consumption decline, but pressure from the Temperance movement helped force a change in the licensing laws, allowing pubs and beerhouses surplus to requirements on social grounds to be closed by magistrates. Nearly ten per cent of the on-licenses existing in 1906 were closed by 1914, largely due to the implementation of the 1904 Licensing Act.

The breweries which prospered in this difficult period were those which had been well-managed during the 1880s and 1890s, prudently buying an estate of public houses and expanding slowly. Robinsons, which had followed precisely this policy, was well placed to take advantage of the decline of badly-managed breweries. While others failed to pay dividends on their shares and had to restructure their companies, William Robinson continued the steady expansion of the Unicorn Brewery, opening a new ale and stout bottling department in 1908, and adding to the Robinson estate, which comprised over thirty houses by 1910. Production climbed from 23,251 barrels (each containing thirty-six gallons at 1,055 degree strength) in 1907 to 34,693 barrels in 1912. This forty-nine per cent growth in output resulted in a sixty-one per cent increase in the total selling value of the six ales produced, which included Old Tom barley wine, first brewed around 1899.

New brewery offices were built around 1913 on the site of Gordon's stay (corset) shop in Lower Hillgate. The shop was

One of Robinson's most treasured possessions, an early Old Tom bottle still with its original contents.

Old Tom in the 30s.

Gordon's stay (corset) shop on Lower Hillgate, where the new brewery offices were built around 1913. The archway still exists, but has been widened to give better access to the brewery yard.

housed in a structure reputedly dating from the fifteenth century, possibly a farm connected with the Lord of the Manor, which eventually came to form the south side of the narrow entrance to the brewery yard. Rebuilding provided both better access and a distinctive frontage for the brewery, which then provided employment for over seventy people. The offices were constructed from red brick with sandstone dressings, and topped by an ornate Dutch gable; the words 'Unicorn Brewery Offices' appeared on the facade.

Ornate stained glass sign rescued from the brewery offices and now displayed in the Unicorn Room at the brewery

Women workers keep the beer flowing during the 1914-18 war years.

THE ROBINSON fleet of horse drays was expanded by the addition of three steam waggons, in spite of a near disaster after a delivery to the New Inn at Dukinfield. Descending the steep hill leading to Stalybridge a steam waggon went out of control and crashed, but fortunately the driver survived.

Steam waggons were used by the brewery for deliveries up till 1920.

The King's Arms, Market Street, Stalybridge, which was founded as a Wine and Spirit Merchants by Joseph Heginbotham and his wife Charlotte, in 1851.

ONE OF the breweries which failed to thrive in the early years of the century was John Heginbotham Ltd of the Borough Brewery, Stalybridge; this company was to become Robinson's first brewery acquisition. The company was founded in 1851 by Joseph Heginbotham, a wine and spirit merchant then living with his wife Charlotte and nephew John Heginbotham at the King's Arms, Market Street in Stalybridge. It appears that Joseph, born in 1813 at Bredbury, died within a few years of establishing the company. Charlotte was running the inn by 1857, and by 1861 John had taken charge and was making a success of the brewing business. He was assisted by the patronage of Samuel Ousey, a coach pro-

The Stalybridge family almanac, 1866.

prietor who lived to the rear of the inn, and who helped make the King's Arms one of the most important coaching inns in Stalybridge.

DURING THE 1870s John Heginbotham bought two other pubs in the centre of Stalybridge, the Freemason's Arms in High Street and the Hare and Hounds in Grosvenor Street; he also opened a wine and spirit merchants store near the King's Arms. His success became evident in 1873, when his family moved from the King's Arms to a house known as The Oaklands, on fashionable Mottram

John Heginbotham, Brewer, Shipper, and Bonder of Wines and Spirits, 47, Market Street, Stalybridge. – The history of this old-established and well-known house dates from the year 1851 ; Mr. John Heginbotham remains sole proprietor and director of its affairs. The premises in Market Street constitute the wine and spirit stores of the concern, and are of commodious dimensions. They contain the general offices of the house, the retail sale department, and large cellars for bottling ales and stout. There is also a fine cellar for the storage of wine in butts, many of which range in capacity from one hundred to four hundred gallons ; other cellars adjoin this for keeping wines, spirits, and liqueurs in bottle; and at the back of the premises there is a large shed for empty bottles and for bottle-washing purposes. The stocks held include all the leading growths and brands of foreign wines, spirits, and liqueurs, with a choice selection of whiskies and foreign spirits. Bass's ale and Guinness's stout are specialities ; and careful attention has been given to the importation of select brands of Havana and other foreign cigars.

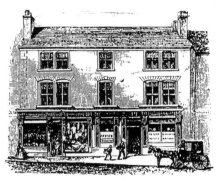

Mr. Heginbotham, in 1888, commenced brewing operations upon a large scale, and has achieved much success in this department. The brewery comprises three extensive blocks of brick buildings, and has a complete equipment of the best modern brewing plant. The product of this establishment enjoys an excellent and well-deserved reputation, and Mr. Heginbotham's various ales and invalid stout form a notable speciality of his business. Altogether, a large number of men, with several horses, lurries, &c., are called into requisition ; and the house owns the "King's Arms" (86, Market Street) and the "Hare and Hounds" (Grosvenor Square), besides other well-known public-houses in Stalybridge and vicinity. The trade is both wholesale and retail, and is of a widespread and influential character. The house enjoys the direct personal attention and supervision of Mr. Heginbotham, who is a member of the Town Council, and much esteemed as an exemplary business man and citizen.

Household names in Stalybridge, around 1887.

Road in the southern outskirts of Stalybridge. John Heginbotham went on to become a town councillor in 1883, and held this position for four years.

THE COMPANY continued to expand, and a new brewery, the Borough Brewery and Mineral Water Works, was built on Borough Street, Stalybridge in 1887. By 1892, Heginbothams owned six licensed houses in Stalybridge. John Heginbotham died at the age of seventy-three on the 7th June 1903, leaving the business in the hands of his four sons: Joseph, John, Ralph and Edward. The firm became a private limited company in April 1908, with John, then aged thirty-five, as chairman.

HOWEVER DISASTER struck the Heginbothams just over four years later. John died on the 17th September 1912 from ptomaine poisoning, a type of food poisoning then thought to be caused by the consumption of decayed meat; in this case, the tragedy was a consequence of eating boiled fowl at a family dinner in York. All six of those present at the meal became seriously ill, and although Mrs Heginbotham and her ten year old son John recovered, her brother-in-law also died.

JOHN HEGINBOTHAM devoted his life to building up the family business, and was held in high esteem in Stalybridge, but after this

Heginbotham Borough Brewery, Stalybridge. The first brewery acquired by Robinson's, in April 1915.

tragedy the company foundered. It went into voluntary liquidation on the 23rd November 1914. William Robinson bought the assets for £11,899 7s 9d on the 1st April 1915. As well as the brewery, the assets included two off-licenses and five public houses. Of the pubs, only the Hare and Hounds in Stalybridge, (now the Grosvenor), still exists.

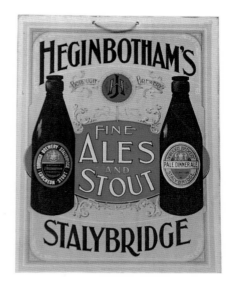

An early Heginbotham advertisement from around 1912.

THE SITE of the Borough Brewery was eventually sold off, leaving Robinsons with an increase in outlets; possibly William Robinson was concerned about surplus brewing capacity at the Unicorn Brewery, as consumption generally declined. Throughout the industry brewing capacity was being rationalised and licensed property bought up, although at a slower rate than before the turn of the century. Sixty-seven breweries were absorbed by other companies between 1900 and 1914. William continued the slow expansion of the company, buying further licensed property including the Horsfield Arms at Bredbury in 1919; the land included in this purchase was later to be the site of the Unicorn Brewery's first plant to be built outside Stockport. A sad footnote to this steady progress was the death in 1918 of Robinson's head brewer, Alfred Munton, after twenty-eight years with the company.

William's eldest son Frederic, one of the first brewers in Britain to obtain a Science Degree.

By 1918, all three of the fourth generation Robinson sons had joined the family business. William's eldest son, Frederic, gained a B.Sc. with honours in chemistry from Manchester Municipal School of Technology, (now the University of Manchester Institute of Science and Technology), in 1911. He was one of the first brewers in Britain to have a science degree, and went on to obtain a master's degree, taking yeast as the subject of his thesis. He was later to be responsible for the company's first laboratory, the erection of a new brewhouse and the introduction of production control into the brewing process.

Brook House, Offerton, July 1916. (Left to right) Priscilla, John Edgar, Frederic, Emma, Cecil, Mabel and William.

FREDERIC ROBINSON LIMITED

ALTHOUGH MANY brewing companies adopted limited liability status, enabling them to raise money through the stock market, in the late nineteenth and early twentieth centuries, Robinsons remained purely a family business. As both the brewing and licensed property aspects of the company expanded, however, it was felt that the finances of the business should be restructured in keeping with its size.

A MEETING was held at Emma Robinson's home, Brook House, Offerton, on the 7th October 1920, when it was decided that the business should become a private limited company, which it has remained to this day. The nominal capital of the new Company was set at £300,000. Only four people attended the meeting: Emma and her son William, as executors of the estate of Frederic, William's son John, who had recently qualified as a solicitor and entered the family business, and solicitor William Johnston.

WILLIAM BECAME Chairman and Managing Director, and on the Monday following the meeting, bought seven public houses for the new company. The first meeting of Frederic Robinson Limited was held on the 4th November 1920; those present were Emma, William and John. John was appointed Secretary and William Johnston became the Company's solicitor; Johnston's firm, now Walls Johnston & Co, still act for Frederic Robinson Limited. A bank account was opened with the Manchester and County Bank Limited, which as the National Westminster Bank Plc remain bankers to the company, and Kidsons Taylor & Co were

A company cheque, signed by William in 1930.

Brook House, Offerton, Frederic and Emma's family home.

(Opposite) William Robinson, Chairman from 1920 until 1933.

appointed auditors; as Kidsons Impey, the firm still retains this function.

On the 18th April 1921, only six months after the business she had done so much to build up became a limited company, Emma died. She had been involved with the family business for six decades.

The early 1920s saw an extensive programme of pub purchases, and the company had to face the twin problems of plummeting beer consumption, (per capita beer consumption in the early 1920s was over one third down on the pre-First World War figure), and a public increasingly attracted to the cinema, radio and sport rather than the public house. There had been no great demand for wartime restrictions on opening hours to be lifted. In these circumstances, only brewers who responded rapidly to the demand for better public houses, a change from the image of urban drinking holes, could hope to prosper.

On the 1st January 1926 William, then Sole Director of Frederic Robinson Limited, appointed his three sons Frederic, John and Cecil to the Board. William specified the conditions under which Emma's grandsons became Directors as follows: 'With such limited powers and duties as I may from time to time define or appoint and at such remuneration as I may fix from time to time. Any Director who I now appoint will also be subject to removal from office at any time.'

Thomas Scholfield, the founder of Scholfield's Brewery, around 1824.

James Scholfield son of Thomas, who expanded the business after his father's death. He was responsible for building the Portland Brewery, which opened in 1865.

Portland Brewery,
ASHTON·under·Lyne
SCHOLFIELD & SON,
BREWERS,

The Highland Laddie, Mossley, where Thomas Scholfield became Innkeeper in 1814. He stayed here for 12 years before moving to the Friendship Inn, Ashton-under-Lyne in 1824.

Scholfields Portland Street Brewery photographed in the Fifties, was Robinson's second major brewery acquisition in 1926.

ROBINSON'S LOOKED to expand and adapt to changes in the market throughout the 1920s, and their second major brewery acquisition was Scholfield's Portland Street Brewery of Ashton-under-Lyne in 1926. Scholfield's was established by Thomas Scholfield around 1824 at the Friendship Inn, Old Street, Ashton-under-Lyne. Thomas was born in Mossley, just north of Stalybridge, in September 1786. Although his parents, James and Betty Scholfield, were members of the licenced trade, Thomas began working life as a joiner. Only after marrying did he become an innkeeper, at the Highland Laddie in Mossley in 1814. Possibly his wife Sarah ran the inn while Thomas continued working as a joiner; this type of arrangement was not uncommon. Their first child, James, was also born in 1814. They stayed at the Highland Laddie for twelve years, moving to Ashton-under-Lyne and erecting the Friendship Inn in 1824. There they began to brew beer for themselves and other local outlets.

Interior of the Friendship Inn, Ashton-under-Lyne, Christmas Day 1826.

THE FRIENDSHIP was the meeting place of the Society of Ancient Shepherds, which was founded by Thomas Scholfield and eleven friends in 1826. It was an organisation similar to the Independent Order of Oddfellows, and grew to a national society with over 80,000 members by the 1870s. Apart from Thomas Scholfield's interest in the activities of the lodge, he was doubtless

*The Old Pack Horse Inn, Audenshaw,
one of Scholfield's many houses.*

pleased with the income generated during the Society's meetings at the inn. Around 1840, James Scholfield left the Friendship to run his own inn, the Southams Arms in Ashton-under-Lyne. He married Mary Coldwell a year later, and their only child Anne was born about 1843.

IN 1849 Sarah Scholfield died and Thomas retired, moving away from the Friendship Inn to nearby Henry Square, where he lived with his youngest daughter. The Friendship was left in the hands

Regulars gather outside The Junction Inn, Ashton-under-Lyne, c.1900.

of James, who expanded the business and ran it with the help of his family. The brewery prospered, and the buildings at the Friendship were increased in size to cope with the demand, but eventually James found it necessary to build an entirely new brewery. Scholfield's Portland Street Brewery (actually on Bentinck Street, Ashton-under-Lyne) was opened in 1865.

THOMAS SCHOLFIELD, founder of the firm, died on the 18th December 1870. In the early 1870s James continued to expand

Distinctive screw-top bottles.

The popular flip-top bottle, used by Scholfield's in the 1920s – now making a comeback.

the tied estate, buying and building public houses. It was clear that James was to have no male heir, and in 1877 Henry Hibbert, who had begun work at the brewery as a bookkeeper in 1860, was appointed brewery manager. James Scholfield retained an active

AS SURE AS PUDDINGS ARE BETTER MADE WITH MILK THAN WITH WATER

SCHOLFIELD'S
MILK STOUT

Brewed under
Letters Patent

Nos. 13528-1908
and 1269-1909

IS BETTER THAN ANY OTHER STOUT

MILK STOUT is not a "fancy" name, and everyone taking it may be assured that EACH PINT BOTTLE ACTUALLY CONTAINS THE ENERGISING CARBO-HYDRATES OF HALF-A-PINT OF PURE MILK in addition to the usual nutriment of Stout.

MILK STOUT is invaluable in cases of Rheumatism, Gout and Indigestion, and for all Invalids.

MILK STOUT SUITS EVERYBODY, 2/- per doz.

BOOKLET giving further particulars and copies of testimonials from all the principal Medical Journals will be sent on receipt of post card

THOS. SCHOLFIELD & SON, Portland Brewery
ASHTON-UNDER-LYNE   Telephone No. 122

An early advertisement for Scholfield's famous Milk Stout.

interest in the business, although still having time and energy enough to become a Justice of the Peace. Hibbert continued to expand the brewery's holdings of licensed property (Scholfield's owned seventeen on-licenses in the Ashton-under-Lyne area and four in Stalybridge by 1892), and the Portland Street Brewery moved again in 1887, into the adjacent Egret Spinning Mill, which was reconstructed as a brewery. James Scholfield died on the 13th December 1894.

HENRY HIBBERT carried on the business until his death in 1897, when it was taken on by Jeffrey Grime, a nephew of James Scholfield. He successfully introduced the famous Milk Stout to the range of Scholfield's ales in 1908, and became managing director of the firm, then known as T. Scholfield & Son, in 1915. The business was registered as a private limited company in 1915, becoming Scholfield's Portland Brewery (Ashton-under-Lyne) Limited. It continued to trade profitably and was active in the wine

The Bull's Head, Old Street, Ashton-under-Lyne, a Scholfield's house that is now demolished.

and spirit trade, but by 1925 Jeffrey Grime, who had no male heir, had reached his sixty-ninth year, and it was therefore decided that the brewery should be sold. The company owned a total of forty-two public houses by this time.

WILLIAM BOUGHT Scholfield's on the 10th February 1926 for the sum of £137,443 5s 10d. The forty-two houses were a very useful addition to the growing Robinson estate, being situated mainly outside the area previously covered, and the wine and spirit business, a new venture for the company, was later developed by Cecil. The brands included Carmen sherry, Don Manuel port and Ye Olde Times rum, all of which continue to this day.

EVEN BEFORE the purchase of Scholfield's and the concentration of brewing in Stockport, the demand for Robinsons ales necessitated upgrading of the brewery plant. In 1925-9 a new brewhouse was built at the Unicorn Brewery under the supervision of Frederic, who equipped it with the most modern plant available, obtained from Robert Morton & Co of Burton upon Trent. The brewhouse was located immediately adjacent to the previous brewery, and its seven storey tower, topped by ornamental stonework including four large red unicorns, is still a landmark in Stockport today.

Jeffrey Grime, nephew of James Scholfield and last owner of the Portland Street Brewery.

TO TAKE up some of the increased brewing capacity, the Robinson Board looked for other possible brewery acquisitions, and in 1929 bought Kay's Atlas Brewery Ltd of Manchester. Kay's originated with the wholesale wine and spirit business Hannay & Dickson, established by David Hannay and William Dickson in 1858 at the Sun Inn, 245 Deansgate, in the centre of Manchester. Their business was successful and soon they expanded into premises on nearby Cross Street. They also bought several licensed houses including three in Salford: the Lord Nelson on Chapel

An early Kay's Atlas embossed bottle.

Street, the Bridge Inn on Broughton Road and the Three Legs of Man on Gravel Lane, Greengate, which is still a Robinson's house today.

THEIR BREWING operation began in 1868 when they purchased the Atlas Buildings on Stockport Road, Longsight, Manchester and converted it into a brewery. During the 1870s Hannay & Dickson greatly increased their holdings of pubs and off-licenses, then sold the thriving business in 1882 to James Kay of Timperley. James Kay had previously been a butter merchant, but left the trade to concentrate on brewing at what became known as Kay's Atlas Brewery. By 1892 Kay's owned eighteen licensed houses in the Manchester area.

Draymen from Kay's Atlas Brewery making one of their many deliveries in the Manchester area.

The motorised Leyland Fleet at the Unicorn Brewery. Left of the picture you can see the old steam waggons. c.1920.

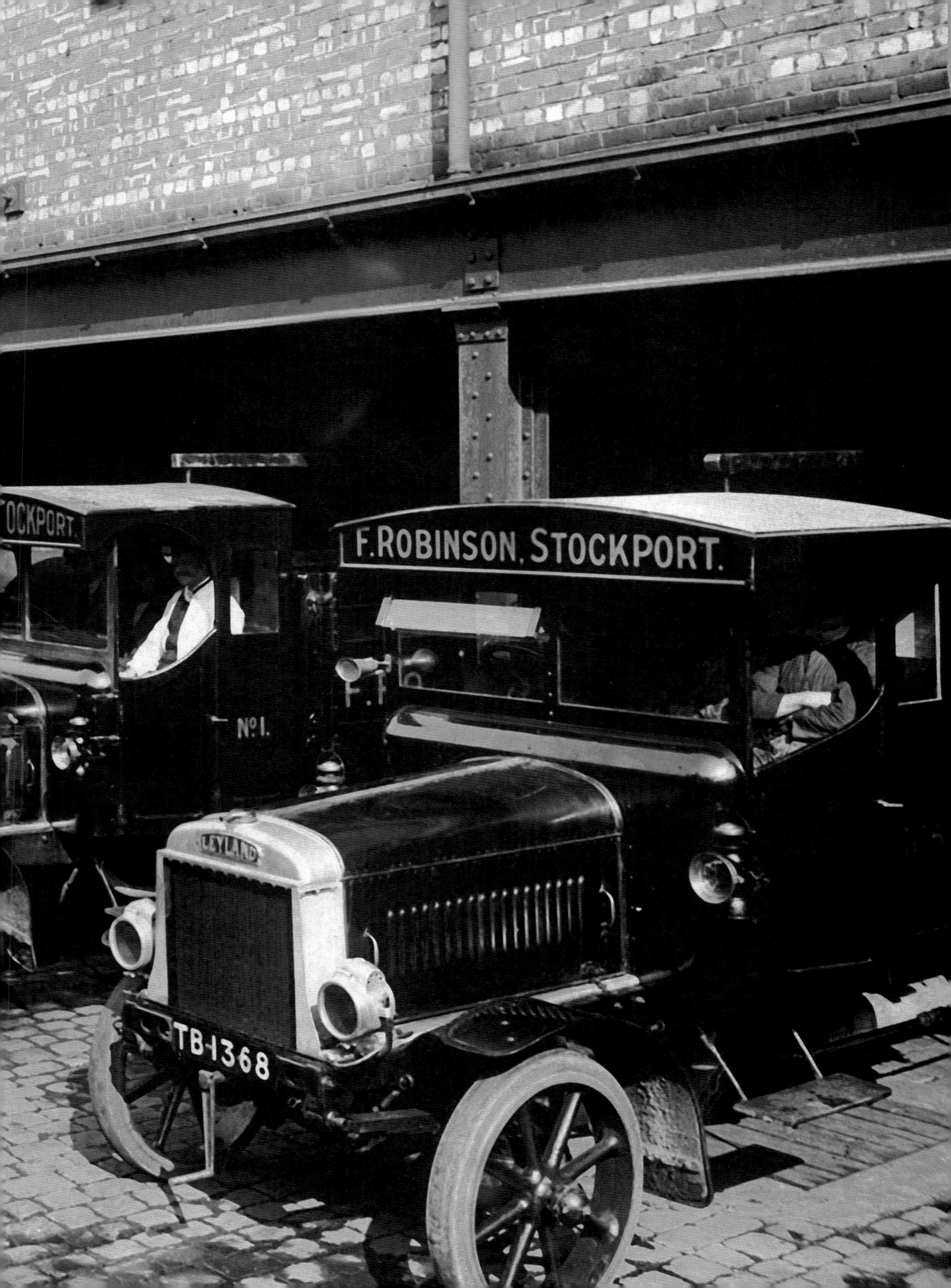

OCKPORT.
F. ROBINSON. STOCKPORT.
No. 1.
LEYLAND
TB 1368

ONE OF the Atlas Brewery's Manchester competitors was Beaumont & Heathcote, who took over the Chorlton-on-Medlock Brewery on Jenkinson Street, near Oxford Street, in 1861. The brewery, which had been in existence since around 1837, was renamed the Standard Brewery, and the business became a limited company about 1890, when its owners were Captain Walter Beaumont and William Heathcote.

SIX YEARS later, Kay's merged with Beaumont & Heathcote Limited, and the resulting company was registered in December 1896 as Kay's Atlas Brewery Limited, with capital of over £200,000. The assets of the new company included 125 licensed houses and a large number of off-licenses. The Standard Brewery was sold off (it became a chocolate factory) and brewing was concentrated at the Atlas Brewery. After many difficult years, during which Kay's estate was reduced in size, the company began to prosper in the 1920s. By the time of the Frederic Robinson takeover in 1929, Kay's owned eighty-six public houses (twenty-six still remain) and forty off-licenses. The Atlas Brewery was closed in 1936. The Robinson delivery fleet was brought up to date at the end of the 1920s by the acquisition of Kay's Thorneycroft waggons and the purchase of Leyland motorised waggons, which enabled the older steam waggon fleet to be phased out.

IMMEDIATELY AFTER the acquisition of Kay's, Robinson's began an intensive programme of public house alteration and refurbishment, carried out under the direction of John. With the addition of Scholfield's wine and spirit business, Cecil was also able to broaden the range of drinks available to Robinson's customers. The building of a modern brewhouse, public house upgrading and increasing customer choice all enabled Robinsons to stay profitable in the difficult 1920s and 1930s. By the early 1930s, average per capita consumption of beer had dwindled to less than half of the pre-First World War figure.

AN EPITAPH TO WILLIAM ROBINSON ESQ, written 1933.

The late Mr William Robinson, in his own quiet, unassuming way, was a fine example of the genuine English type of gentleman. Strong alike in his direct and practical speech and in his silences, he had the true Englishman's dislike of weakness and inefficiency. The keen and brilliantly successful businessman was also the well-groomed and cheerful gentleman. Seldom seen without a rose or an orchid or a carnation in his button-hole, he was kindness itself to many a poor unfortunate, who did not even know the name of his benefactor.

John Robinson, Chairman from 1933 until 1978, and above with his wife Gwendolen and sons, from left Dennis, Peter and David, outside the George & Dragon, Holmes Chapel, on the occasion of the Annual General Meeting, Thursday 4th June 1970.

THE INTER-WAR years saw many changes for the Robinson family as well as the company. John married Gwendolen Evans of Streatham on the 17th April 1926, and their first child, Peter, was born in 1931. Two more sons followed: Dennis, born in 1933, and David, born in 1937; the fifth generation of Robinsons. William, still Chairman of the company, died on the 25th January 1933; this was a great loss to both family and company, as he had served the family business for fifty-five years. He was succeeded as Chairman by his son John, and under his direction Robinson's continued its steady progress through the difficult 1930s depression.

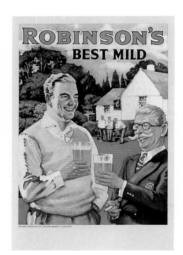

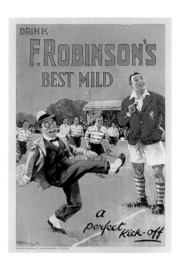

A series of nostalgic postcards featuring publicity material from the
30s and 40s, illustrated by H. Harris.

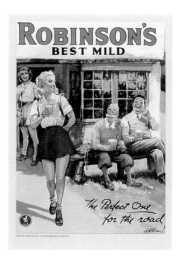

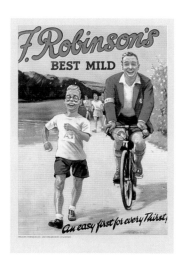

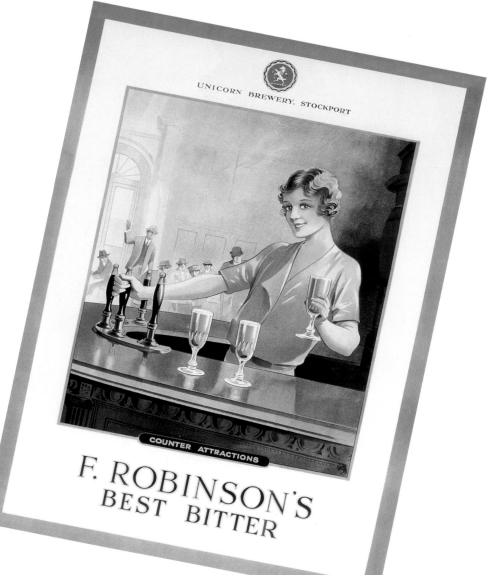

A Robinson's Best Bitter
advertisement from the 1930s.

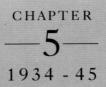

COUNTRY PUBS

Although Robinson's began life as a town brewery, catering largely for customers in Stockport and later in the Manchester conurbation, by the 1930s its image was undergoing a radical transformation. The sign of the Unicorn began to appear further

afield, notably on a series of picturesque country inns which appealed to a far wider range of potential customers than the urban pubs. John, the new Chairman, concentrated on pub acquisitions in rural areas, wishing to attract the family clientele which he saw as vital to the future success of the brewery. This policy contrasted sharply with that of many of the company's competitors, but proved a great success.

An early photograph of the Crown at Hawk Green, which was purchased by the Robinsons in June 1949.

HAWK GREEN,
MARPLE.

AMONGST THE pubs bought by Robinsons in the 1930s was the Bulls Head at Ashford-in-the-Water, near Bakewell, deep in the heart of Derbyshire's Peak District. The inn, still in Robinson ownership, is both picturesque country pub and typical vernacular building, complete with stone slab roof. In the attractive Cheshire

The Bulls Head, Ashford-in-the-Water.

village of Prestbury, Robinsons bought and still own the Legh Arms (or Black Boy), and the Admiral Rodney – now known as the Ye Olde Admiral Rodney – which is another lovely vernacular building with a fine set of chimneystacks. The Legh Arms dates back to the early fifteenth century and gave shelter to Bonnie Prince Charlie on his journey south in 1745.

THE LEGH ARMS

The Legh Arms, pictured below in 1900, and right as it looks today, first saw life as an Inn way back in 1423, when it was known as the Saracen's Head, in commemoration of the Holy Crusade.

In 1719 a new sign was painted, the painter making a mistake by painting a Negro's head – so the Inn was known successively as the Blackamoor's Head and the Black Boy, and it was under the latter name that the Inn played host to Bonnie Prince Charlie on his way south during the 1745 rebellion.

A long and proud history indeed, with worthy traditions well maintained to this day. The Legh Arms became a part of the Robinson Estate in 1939.

The Legh Arms, Prestbury circa 1900.

ALTHOUGH MANY fine pubs were purchased in the 1930s, there was one sad loss - the original Unicorn Inn. Robinson's continued to buy up land adjacent to the Unicorn Brewery site throughout the 1930s to provide room for expansion, and as part of this process, on the 31st December 1935 the Unicorn itself, still a functioning public house, was closed and demolished. The building was over 200 years old, and it was a rather unhappy end for the pub which provided the inspiration for the well known sky blue and white unicorn motif, as well as the brewery name.

On yer bike! Regulars gather outside the Bulls Head, Ashford in the Water, at the start of the local Penny Farthing Rally, 1885.

THE DUSTY MILLER

The Dusty Miller is situated on the Llangollen Branch (formerly Ellesmere Branch) of the Shropshire Union Canal at Bridge No. 20, opposite the Wrenbury Mill Basin, Wrenbury, Cheshire.

Formerly a working mill dating back to the 16th Century, the first building was under the ownership of the nearby Combermere Abbey; it had an underpass wheel with the building straddling the River Weaver.

With the opening of the canal at the beginning of the 19th Century, the second building was erected in its present day position with a side wheel again worked by the adjacent river Weaver. It ceased as a working mill at the beginning of the 20th Century and became a collection point for locally grown produce which would be taken to Manchester Market in two days by 'Fly' boats. Between the wars it became a cheese storage warehouse and, in its latter days, a storage mill for the then working mill opposite.

It became derelict in 1970 and was converted into Licensed premises in 1977. The Dusty Miller is easily accesible by canal and road and is delightfully situated on the canal side in picturesque rural surroundings on the outskirts of Wrenbury, one of Cheshire's prettiest villages.

An early photograph of the Mill where the Dusty Miller now stands, you can just see the Draw Bridge in the foreground.

THE ALVANLEY ARMS

This early photograph shows that a drive out to the Alvanley Arms, Cotebrook, near Tarporley was as popular at the turn of the century as it is today. The building has changed little over the years, as can be seen from the more recent photograph overleaf.

YE OLDE ADMIRAL RODNEY

The Admiral Rodney is a cottage-style Inn of great character – as intimate as a ship's cabin, it was purchased by Robinsons in 1939. In the early 1700s, when the Inn was built, the main road through Prestbury forded the River Bollin, and passed along Pearl Street to Adlington. With the advent of the new bridge in 1850 came a new road, passing through the back garden of the Admiral Rodney – so the back became the front. But habit dies hard, and most of today's regulars still enter by the old front door.

Top left clockwise:

THE ALVANLEY ARMS
Cotebrook, Tarporley

THE BULLS HEAD
Church Street, Glossop

THE WAGGON AND HORSES
Eaton, Congleton

YE OLDE CHESHIRE CHEESE
Longnor, Derbyshire

THE WAGGON AND HORSES

(Main Picture) Early morning deliveries at the Waggon and Horses at Matley, on the road between Mottram and Stalybridge, circa 1890. Originally called 'The Sawmill Inn', it was built as a farmhouse in 1663 and opened as a tavern and coaching inn in 1789. The pub shown above in a recent photograph was bought by Robinsons in 1910.

THE RAILWAY

Today it is still easy to recognise the Railway Inn on Ashley Road, Hale, from the photograph taken at around the turn of the century.

The pub is just one of a number of Robinson's pubs that are reported to have their own resident ghost, with the Railway's being that of the late Mary Holt.

Mary was apparently the wife of a previous licensee, who died in an electrical fire some three generations ago. Several sightings have been made of Mary, mainly on the first floor landing of the premises which as legend has it, was where Mary tried to seek her exit from the blaze.

It is interesting to note though, that those who are supposed to have seen the poor lady always report the distinct smell of lavender water, and recently it has been confirmed by a visiting relative that Mary's favourite scent was "4711", which just happens to smell of........lavender.

Bottom left clockwise:

NEW HALL INN
Lowside, Bowness-on-Windermere

KINGFISHER INN
Crown Street, Cockermouth, Cumbria

QUEENS HEAD
Hawkshead, Ambleside, Cumbria

QUEEN'S
HEAD

VACANCIES

'QUEEN'S HEAD'
Bar Lunches
Served
12.00-2.15 pm
12.00-2.30 pm
(SUNDAYS)

Evening Bar Meals
6.15-9.30 pm

A la carte Dinners
6.45-9.00 pm

EGON
RONAY'S
GUIDES

HARTLEYS   HARTLEYS   HARTLEYS

THE SMOKER

The Smoker at Plumley was purchased by Robinsons in 1948, and is probably Cheshire's most famous Inn. It is situated on the ancient Roman Watling Street, and has served its wayfarers since Elizabethan times.

The name is not, as might have been supposed, connected with Sir Walter Raleigh and 'the weed', but derives from a later historical figure, the first Lord de Tabley, who raised the Cheshire Yeomanry against the threat of Napoleonic invasion. He owned a white charger, bred by the Prince Regent, which under the name of The Smoker raced nineteen times, won 12, was second three times, third twice and unplaced twice.

The Smokers' reputation now is not for racing, but for English and Continental cuisine of a very high order.

An early photograph of Smoker Corner, circa 1890.

Regulars gather outside The Smoker, Plumley, as the local Rally prepares for the 'Off', circa 1900.

THE SYCAMORE

In the past, the hanging baskets outside the Sycamore Inn at Parwich near Ashbourne have received more than their fair share of attention.

For it's here that 'Dyllis' the local duck decided to lay her eggs. Ignoring the landlord's carefully nurtured Pansies, Dyllis successfully hatched 14 of her 18 eggs. Throughout most of the year, Parwich is just a sleepy village nestling quietly in the Derbyshire countryside. Every Tuesday, the Sycamore doubles as the Doctors Surgery with patients waiting in the Dining room or on cold winter days by the open fire near the bar.

Once a year though the pub becomes the focal point for the annual summer festival culminating in the Oddfellows March followed by a spit roast. Often this great occasion coincides with Dyllis's hatchings, always staying exactly 28 days, she often sits blissfully unaware as some 500 villagers march by.

The Sycamore Inn, circa 1900. It was purchased by Robinson's in 1992.

*Keeping all her eggs in one basket,
Dyllis sits amongst the remains of the
pansies, blissfully unaware of village
life going on all around her.*

Clockwise from left:

RISING SUN
High Street, Tarporley

GAZELLE HOTEL
Menai Bridge, Anglesey

SQUARE & COMPASS
Darley Dale, Matlock

THE CHURCH HOUSE

Regulars in The Church House, Buglawton, Congleton, continued drinking ale during this fire, which destroyed the original thatch in 1953. Throughout the afternoon firemen fought to control the blaze, until around 10.30 pm, when thirsts and flames were both well and truly quenched.

The original Church House, Old Buxton Road. The name and licence were transferred to the present building (top) a few years before Robinson's acquisition in 1929.

THE CAT AND FIDDLE

Sir Henry Royce (centre, in white), sat at the wheel of his Rolls Royce Silver Ghost, outside The Cat and Fiddle between Buxton and Macclesfield, c.1900. Situated at an altitude of 1,690 ft, it is the second highest pub in England, and offers the tourist unsurpassed views. Sir Henry and his team periodically used the surrounding terrain to road test the world famous Rolls Royce cars.

High above Macclesfield, The Cat and Fiddle as seen today.

THE BULLS HEAD

(Main Picture) The Bulls Head, Hale Barns circa 1890, the building's original core dates back to the 18th century. It became a Robinsons Pub in 1967 and later in 1994 after a stunning conversion (above) won the Publican Pub Design of the year award.

*A pint of 'Robbies' was the Hero in
Stockport during the Second World War.*

THE ADVENT of the Second World War brought difficulties for the brewing industry in the form of restrictions on brewing materials, increases on beer duty and shortages of labour and good quality raw materials. As a result, many brewers resorted to brewing weaker ales, and total production actually increased over the wartime period. It was fortunate that the Unicorn Brewery and all but one of the Robinsons pubs escaped direct hits by bombing; the unlucky house was the Railway in Wilburn Street, Salford.

BODDINGTONS BREWERIES LTD of Manchester were, however, hit by enemy action on the night of the 22nd December 1940, when their Strangeways Brewery was bombed, leaving only the bottling stores intact. Robinsons were amongst the twenty-two breweries which helped out Boddingtons while the brewery was being rebuilt, which took until August 1941. Boddingtons took casks to the Unicorn Brewery to be filled, and then delivered the substitute ale to their own customers.

DESPITE THE war, Robinsons pressed ahead with their pub acquisition policy, and in May 1943 purchased the first house of what was to become a substantial Welsh estate, now comprising thirty-one houses. The pub involved in this adventurous decision was the Black Lion Hotel in the quiet village of Llanfair Talhaiarn, near Abergele; it is still a Robinson's house today.

*The Black Lion Hotel, Llanfair Talhaiarn.
Robinson's first pub acquisition in Wales.*

A FIRE on the night of Saturday the 27th November 1943 ensured that the Unicorn Brewery did not come through the war totally unscathed. It was 5.00pm when Mr Arthur Wood, Robinson's surveyor working late in the Building Department, first saw signs of a fire in the brewery complex and called the National Fire Service. The building was ablaze from the third floor upwards and it took three hours to bring the fire under control. Firemen fought the fire from precarious positions on ladders and adjacent buildings, and

Divisional Officer H. Ryder (left) was in charge of the N.F.S. Units operating, and during the height of the fire.

three of them were injured by a falling beam. It was midnight before the blaze was totally extinguished, but the fire had been prevented from spreading to the new brewhouse, where the gleaming copper brewing vessels might have been destroyed.

ALTHOUGH IT was a spectacular fire, there were no serious casualties, and even the office cat was rescued by a member of Robinsons staff. Most of the contents of the offices remained intact, and the vital stocks of malt escaped significant damage. The brewery was able to restart production within a week, and supplied customers from stock in the intervening few days. The Chairman later paid personal tribute to the men of the National Fire Service for their selfless efforts.

'Ginger'

ROBBIES ABLAZE!

Stockport Brewery Ablaze —
Saturday November 27th, 1943.
100 N.F.S. men show their mettle.

The flaming upper stories of the old brew house, the billowing clouds of smoke white in the light of the N.F.S. spotlights, made a spectacular sight. N.F.S. men fought the biggest fire in Stockport for some years. On Saturday night, over 100 N.F.S. men battled for nearly three hours before the outbreak was brought under control.

N.F.S. men perched precariously 100 foot in the air. Inside the building they fought to keep the blaze from the new brew house. A few yards from the gleaming copper beer vats they handled the blaze. The fire was discovered by firewatchers shortly after 5 p.m., and when the N.F.S. men arrived they found the whole of the third and upper storeys well ablaze. The fire was under control by 8 p.m., but it was not extinguished until midnight.

High tribute to the work of the N.F.S. men has been paid by Mr. Edgar (Sir John) Robinson. They were marvellous he said, and saved us considerable expense. He explained that the brewery would be in production by the middle of the week, and they had sufficient stock to meet customers demands.

Casualties in the fire were few, only 3 N.F.S. men required First Aid.

The cause is still a mystery. The last fire was in September 1941 in the new brew house.

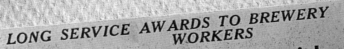

LONG SERVICE AWARDS TO BREWERY WORKERS

Robinsons' Cherish Their Employees' Loyalty

ELEVEN employees with a total of 310 years' service with Frederic Robinson Ltd., Stockport brewers, received gifts including inscribed watches, at the staff dinner in Lyme Hall, on Thursday, last week.

Miss M. Curtis, who completed 25 years' service, also received a silver tea service as a wedding present.

Proposing the toast "Staff Loyalties," Mr J. E. Robinson said "we are living in an age of continually changing values, but our loyalties remain unchanged."

Responding, Mr W. A. Wood said: "I am happy to have the opportunity of expressing to the directors the thanks of the 'people in the vineyard and hopfield.'"

GRIT AND DETERMINATION

Mr A. Radcliffe, who has 52 years' service with the firm, proposing the toast "The House of Robinson," said: "Let us pay tribute to those who toiled with grit and determination and held the fort in the past; to those who valiantly hold the fort and keep the flag flying today; and to those reinforcements round the corner who will be called upon to guide our destiny in the future.

"For years the house of Robinson has been controlled by gentlemen endowed with wisdom to comprehend; judgment to define; courteous in manner and steady and firm in principle.

"Loyalty and service will continue to merit the confidence and esteem of the directors. Let us hand down to those who come

after us a legacy of efficiency."

LOYALTY APPRECIATED

Responding, Mr F. Robinson said the directors appreciated the employees' loyalty, which would always be cherished.

Mr W. Cecil Robinson proposed the toast to the guests and Lt.-Col. K. B. Taylor, O.B.E., responded.

Mr J. W. Roy was the toastmaster, and the M.C.s for dancing were Mr J. Pritchard and Miss E. Sayner.

Recipients of long service awards were:

Messrs J. Faulkner (52) managed house department, of Bramhall Lane, Stockport; J. Bardsley (34), foreman, of Cambridge Street, Heaviley; J. Higginbotham (32), mechanic, of School Street, Cheadle Heath; H. E. Wood (27), cashier, of Curzon Road, Offerton; W. A. Wood (27), surveyor, of Green Lane, Hazel Grove; H. R. Grimes (27), wine and spirit stores manager, of Broadoak Road, Ashton; T. Redfern (27), traffic department, of Tenby Road, Cheadle Heath; H. B. Swann (26), transport engineer, of Compstall Road, Marple Bridge; H. A. Whitehead (25), sales analysis, of Porlock Close, Woodbank, Stockport, and Mrs M. Edwards (25), director's secretary of Dial Road, Stockport, and Miss M. Curtis.

Margaret Thatcher, obviously enjoying her visit to the Brewery in June 1983.

Left: Directors photographed with the long service award recipients. Back row, left to right: Mrs F Robinson, Mr F Robinson, Mrs J E Robinson, Mr J E Robinson, Miss P M J Robinson, Mr W Cecil Robinson. Middle row: Mr H Whitehead, Mr W A Wood, Mr J Redfern, Mr J Faulkner, Mr J Bardsley. Front Row: Mr H E Wood, Mr J Higginbotham, Mrs M Edwards, Mr H R Grime, Mr H B Swann.

Brewers' chief chemist retires

Mr English (right) receives his farewell gift from Mr Frederic Robinson. Sir John Robinson looks on. LY421

A MAN with the record of spending all his working life in the service of one firm, retired on Friday, and an informal presentation was held at the works he has seen expand since he was a lad of 15.

He is Mr Joe English (65), of 5, Hazelwood Road, Woodsmoor, the chief chemist of Messrs. Frederic Robinson's Ltd., Unicorn Brewery, Stockport.

It was in June, 1915, that Mr English started work with the firm, and after studying at Stockport and Manchester technical colleges, became connected with the scientific side of the trade.

A silver bowl and a silver cigarette box were presented to Mr English on behalf of the directors, by Mr Frederic Robinson, joint managing director, after a short speech by his brother, Sir John Robinson, chairman and joint managing director.

Mr J. M. P. Lee, who is to succeed Mr English, presented his former chief with a pair of binoculars and leather case, and from the staff as a whole, and from the laboratory staff he presented a stainless steel carving dish and a carving set.

Mr. JOSEPH ENGLISH samples his last glass of beer on Friday, after being chief chemist and beer taster for 30 years at Robinsons Brewery.

ENDS 30 YEARS TASTING BEER

Friday will go down as a big day in the annals of Robinsons, the Stockport family brewery concern.

Late-arrival as employees and five Robinsons, representing two generations, gathered for a farewell presentation was Mr. Peter Robinson who had been in Manchester to present a gold brooch to Britain's top landlady, who keeps a Robinson house. (see story below).

The presentation was to Mr. Joseph English, chief chemist and beer taster since 1935 and an employee for more than 50 years.

After the ceremony—and toasts in sherry—Mr. English (65), of Hazelwood-road, Woodsmoor, walked over to his laboratory to taste his last glass of beer.

"We check every batch of beer from the water and raw materials right through every stage but taste is the ultimate test," he said.

"I don't think people realise how much trouble we take, but they would certainly know if the beer wasn't right."

Chairman Peter Robinson looks on as Margaret and Dennis Thatcher sign the visitors book after their visit to the Brewery in June 1983.

Workers pause for a quick photo,
Bell's Brewery, Hempshaw Lane.

HENRY BELL AND SIR JOHN ROBINSON

AFTER THE war years, and as government restrictions began to ease, Robinson's continued with its pub maintenance and upgrading programme. The company also sought to carry on the expansion of its brewing activities, but choice in the matter of mergers or takeovers was limited locally to the remaining two competitors in Stockport, Richard Clarke & Co Ltd of the Reddish Brewery, and Bell & Co Ltd. The position of Robinson's as the major brewer in north Cheshire was confirmed by the purchase of Bell's in 1949; Clarke's was taken over by Boddingtons in 1963, and ceased to brew.

The Hempshaw Brook Brewery.

THE BREWING business which was to become Bell & Co Ltd began life in 1835, when Stockport brushmaker Avery Fletcher bought a piece of land in Hempshaw Lane, less than a mile from Lower Hillgate, and on it built a small brewhouse. The first brew from the Hempshaw Brook Brewery was produced in March 1836, and Fletcher's ale and porter must have been popular, as he was able to extend the brewhouse a short time later. The new brewhouse cost around £4,000 to build and was the largest in the area outside Manchester.

An outing from the Finger Post, Hempshaw Lane, Offerton c1900. Originally a Bells pub, it was purchased by Robinson's in 1949.

AVERY FLETCHER continued brewing at Hempshaw Brook for the next few years, but by the mid-1840s the property was in the hands of his two trustees, who came from Staveley, near Chesterfield. They left the disposal of the brewery to one W. Gregory, also from Staveley, who came up with the idea of a lottery. Legal complications were avoided by selling copies of a fine art engraving at a guinea each, every purchaser being presented with a free lottery ticket. The draw was held in Sheffield in February 1850, supervised by a committee on which sat local brewers Thomas Berry, Thomas Birks, the Tennant brothers and R. Trusswell. The result of this fascinating procedure, including the winners of the subsidiary cash prizes, is not recorded, but towards the end of 1850 the Hempshaw Brook Brewery came under the control of Yorkshiremen Joseph Smith and Henry Bell.

The poster used by W. Gregory to advertise his ingenious way of disposing of the Hempshaw Brook Brewery, c.1850.

JOSEPH SMITH was a Sheffield brewer from the firm of A. H. Smith & Co of the Eldon Brewery, founded in 1832 (and taken over by Tennant Brothers in 1915). It appears that Joseph Smith supplied the brewing expertise whilst Henry Bell provided the finance. Henry Bell, from Pocklington near York, had farming interests in Northallerton and did not move to Stockport until 1862. The partnership traded as Smith & Bell, with Smith bringing in Thomas Fearn from Sheffield to be both brewer and manager of the brewery. Thomas Fearn produced their first brew at Hempshaw Brook on the 11th March 1851, the initial output being twenty-two barrels per week.

The Mash Tun at Bells Brewery, c.1908.

THE JOINT venture proved to be a great success, and by the 1860s the brewery was working to capacity supplying a growing number of local pubs and off-licenses. In 1872, Barnsley's Tannery, almost opposite the brewery, came on the market, and was bought

Henry Bell Senior 1825 - 1891, the Founder of Bell and Co Ltd.

by Smith & Bell for conversion to a brewery. The old brewery, with its excellent well water, remained in service. Later that year Joseph Smith retired, leaving Henry Bell, by now a resident of Greek Street, Stockport, as Chairman of Bell & Co Ltd, as the company then became known. Brewer Thomas Fearn's son George joined the firm in the same year. Henry Bell, a JP, became Mayor of Stockport in 1877.

IN 1886, after the retirement of Henry Bell and the death of Thomas Fearn at the age of seventy, a new company partnership was announced. It comprised of Henry's three sons Henry, Alfred and Thomas with Captain George Fearn. Henry Bell senior died in 1891, aged sixty-six. Under Henry Bell junior, Bell's prospered, and by 1892 owned forty-four on-licenses in the Stockport area, more than any other firm. The company also had a strong presence in the Manchester area, with thirty-two houses, in Derbyshire, particularly around Chapel-en-le-Frith and Swadlincote, and elsewhere in Cheshire.

BELL'S MADE £31,000 profit in 1896, and became a limited company in November 1898, with a share capital of £280,000. In 1900, Chairman Henry Bell stated the company's intention of building a new brewery, but nothing came of this except the construction of a new bottling plant in 1909. Finally, in 1926 the company decided to build a new brewery on the old site, as parts of the old brewery were becoming unsafe and the plant was outdated. Building work caused production difficulties for Bell's, as the second brewery (in the old tannery) struggled to maintain the necessary output alone.

THE NEW brewery opened in 1930, covering an area of over 9,000 square yards; it was designed by the head and second brewers with Henry Bell junior. The young Henry Bell took a brewing course at the University of Birmingham and was articled to Stretton's Derby Brewery before beginning work at Bell's. In 1932 the

The White Hart, London Road, Hazel Grove (circa 1890) was a Bell's Pub until it was purchased by Robinson's in 1949.

company was badly affected by the depression and the imposition of increased beer duty; output dropped by twenty-two per cent and plans for modernising licensed houses were shelved. Profitability improved slightly during the late 1930s, but the company was hard hit by the death of Chairman Henry Bell on the 26th January 1943.

HENRY BELL was in his eighty-fourth year, but still worked although incapacitated by blindness. He served two terms as mayor of Stockport, from 1906 to 1908, and was a member of the Town Council for seventeen years. He was appointed a County Magistrate in 1892 and presided over the courts for thirty-nine years, and was a great philanthropist, presenting land to the town for use as open space, and supporting such causes as the Stockport Infirmary. He was a lacrosse and rugby player when a young man,

THE TOWNMAKER No. 12

Alderman Henry Bell and Mrs Bell, Mayor and Mayoress, in procession with the Prince and Princess of Wales, to celebrate the opening of Stockport Town Hall, July 7th 1908.

Mr. Henry Bell

anyone who has lived in ckport for a decade or to write down a list of is men of the town and is little doubt that high te list will be the name f Bell,

h he died in 1943, Henry work for Stockport is alked about when volunservice is discussed.

d at Stockport Grammar ; he entered his father's ry firm for a decade or chairman of Messrs. Bell Co. Ltd. He entered local es in the late 1800s, and the Conservatives took ol of the council in 1900 s one of the first Conser- aldermen to be appoin- or many years.

s the chairman of the ce committee and served vor from 1906 to 1908, the ght of his term of office the visit of the then e and Princess of Wales, King George V and Queen who came to open the hall in 1908.

Bell was appointed a y magistrate in 1892, and 3 years presided over the s. He was appointed a y Lieutenant of Cheshire 6.

a great interest in edu- and Stockport Grammar l where he was made a oor in 1896, and for many vice-chairman of the

many men who have d in this series, Henry vas a supporter of Stock- nfirmary, on whose board

he served for 50 years. Stockport Savings Bank was another interest near to his heart. He was elected a manager in 1893, and was chairman of the board of management from 1919 to 1941.

He was also one of the prime movers in the establishment of the Stockport centre of the St John Ambulance Brigade, being its first chairman. He presented the Emily Bell Hut, Cheadle Heath, to the association in memory of his wife.

A great musician and music lover, Henry Bell was one of the town's leaders in this field. He played the organ at Tiviot Dale Methodist Church, where he was a trustee, for more than 50 years, and he was one of the chief supporters of Stockport Vocal Union.

One of the great days of the year for him was the Vernon Park Open Air Musical Festival.

His love for Stockport was not only shown in his work for the various organisations but also in his benevolence. He gave the land for Cale Green Park, and before his death presented Heathfield, his home, to the town. This is now the annexe of Stockport High School for Girls.

When he died on January 26, 1943, Henry Bell had been blind for some years. An appreciation in the 'Advertiser' at that time read: "Henry Bell leaves behind him a shining example of public service and a fragrant memory of work well and unostentatiously done. Henry Bell was one of nature's gentlemen".

Robinson - Bell Share Deal Goes Through

THE "Advertiser" was authoritatively informed yesterday that the percentage of shares in Bell and Co. Ltd., Hempshaw Brook Brewery, Stockport, available to be bought by Frederic Robinson, Ltd., Unicorn Brewery, Stockport, is acceptable to the directors of the latter firm, whose offer to buy the shares closed yesterday.

This means that Frederic Robinson, Ltd., will take over control of Bell's brewery.

At an extraordinary general meeting of the shareholders of Bell's brewery on Monday, the compensation to be paid to the directors by Frederic Robinson Ltd., was agreed at £22,500.

This sum is to be apportioned as follows:—

As directors: Mr L. W. Ashover £2,100, Mr H. Bell £1,800, Mr M. Bateman, J.P. £1,800 Major P. Carrington Peirce £1800.

As managing director, Mr L. W. Ashover £10,000.

As brewery manager, Mr H Bell £5,000.

These payments do not affect the general shareholders of Bell and Co.

and was also a great lover of music and a skilful organist; he was organist at Tiviot Dale Methodist Church for over fifty years. The writer of his obituary in the Stockport Advertiser felt that Henry Bell could be justly described as the Grand Old Man of Stockport.

DURING HENRY Bell's last years, talks took place between Bell's and Richard Clarke's Reddish Brewery with a view to possible amalgamation. Clarke's may have been in a better financial position than Bell's in the early 1940s, but the talks were discontinued on Henry Bell's death. After the relaxation of wartime restrictions, Bell's decided to re-equip the bottling plant, a process completed by 1947. The company was still in poor financial health, however, and in January 1949 an offer was made for its shares. The source of the offer was initially unidentified, but later turned out to be Robinson's. Bell's share capital was £280,000 made up of equal numbers of £1 ordinary and preference shares. The Bell's Board felt the share offer to be such that it ought to be considered by the shareholders.

AFTER TALKS with Bell's the takeover went through on the 25th March 1949, and Robinson's sent out cheques totalling approximately £65,000 to the shareholders of Bell's who had agreed to the offer. Robinson's bought 134,781 ordinary shares and 8,020 preference shares at £4 15s and £1 7s 6d respectively, enough to give them control. The assets of Bell's, valued at £1,056,398, included the brewery, 155 pubs and off-licenses, and a considerable number of delivery vehicles.

THE BELL'S purchase was the biggest to be undertaken by Robinson's, and it left the company as the largest brewer in north Cheshire. Slowly the Bell's insignia began to disappear from pubs, but because of the need to supply the increased number of licensed houses, Bell's brewery remained in production. Bell's bottling plant took on the bottling of proprietary brands, whilst

BIRTHDAY HONOURS LIST

Brewer gets Knighthood

IN the Birthday Honours to-day (Thursday) the Queen conferred a knighthood upon Mr. John Edgar Robinson, Chairman of Frederic Robinson Ltd., the brewers, of Stockport. The honour is for "political and public services in Cheshire."

Mr. Robinson, who lives at Wellfield, Dean Row, Wilmslow, is Deputy President of Knutsford Division Conservative and Unionist Association.

Other honours include the C.B.E. for Mr. Fred Williamson, Chairman of the North West Area Traffic Commissioners, who lives at Riparo, Fletcher-drive, Disley, and Professor Geoffrey Gee, lecturer in chemistry at Manchester University, of 4 Park-road, Cheadle Hulme.

The M.B.E. is awarded to Mr. John Green, Traffic Manager of the North Western Road Car Company, who lives at 36 Tatton - road South, Heaton Moor, and Miss Edith Dorothy Abraham, of Brentwood Recuperative Centre, Marple: the B.E.M. (Military) for Sgt. James Higginbotham, of the R.A.F. Regiment, who comes from Stockport.

Mr. Robinson has been Chairman of Frederic Robinson Ltd. since 1943. He was one of five prominent Conservatives called together after the war by Mr P S Radcliffe with the object of re-forming the Wilmslow Polling District branch of the Knutsford Division Conservative and Unionist Association.

He was president of Stockport Chamber of Commerce in 1947, and has been a member of its Council since 1943. He is an Income Tax Commissioner for Stockport, a member of the Board of Managers of the Stockport and District Savings Bank, and a Trustee of the Ephraim Hallam Charity.

Chairman of the Chester and North Wales Brewers' Association since 1949, he was appointed vice-chairman of the Manchester and District Brewers' Society last year.

He has been a director of Stockport County Football Club since 1931.

He is married with three sons — two of whom are in the family business and a third is completing his National Service.

Mr. Robinson has lived in Wilmslow since 1934, moving to the village from nearby Bramhall.

(Right) Wilmslow's new knight Sir John and Lady Robinson after the investiture at Buckingham Palace 1958.

Robinson's own brands continued to be bottled at the Unicorn Brewery. However, it was soon found that operating from two sites was a costly exercise, and brewing eventually ceased at Bell's in 1968.

MANY OF the properties acquired from Bell's were found to be in poor repair, and this situation was remedied by a programme of investment and refurbishment which continued throughout the 1950s. External advertising on the improved houses was restrained, in keeping with normal company policy.

IN AUTUMN 1953 Dennis Robinson joined the Company, becoming the first of the fifth generation of Robinson's in the firm; at that time the Board of Directors consisted of Chairman John Robinson and his brothers Frederic and Cecil. Unfortunately ill health was to limit the duties of Frederic. John's eldest son, Peter, joined the company as Company Secretary in January 1957, having qualified as a solicitor.

ONE MEANS by which the Directors kept abreast of all developments at the Unicorn Brewery was their habit of personally opening all the post; the present Directors continue to do this. In the early 1950s the brewery offices consisted of a number of small rooms heated by open fires, entered through a door to the side of the main yard entrance. At that time clerks still worked at steeply inclined wooden desks.

IN 1958, John became Sir John when he received the accolade of a knighthood, bestowed at the first investiture to be undertaken by Prince Philip, Duke of Edinburgh. It was a recognition of his work in political and public service in Cheshire. It crowned a quarter century of success for Sir John, in public life, as Chairman, and as a family man whose sons were now beginning to play their part in Robinson's.

—7—

EXPANSION AT BREDBURY

THE EARLY 1960's saw Robinson's again extending their estate, this time by building rather than acquisition. Amongst the new Robinson houses were the Cheshire Cat at Brinnington, the March Hare on a new estate in Ashton-under-Lyne, and the Pied Piper on an overspill estate at Little Hulton.

THE BREWING industry at this time was beginning to feel the effects of the concentration of output in the hands of a few national concerns; by 1963, the five largest brewing companies accounted for half the industry's output. The number of breweries continued to decline, dropping from 6,447 in 1900 to 358 at the start of the 1960's. It was a harsh climate for the medium-sized companies, and in 1962 Robinson's made two of the fifth generation of the family, Peter and Dennis, Directors, to help the firm remain competitive. Sir John's third son, David, also joined the Company in 1962, and with finance being directed into production invest-ment, made one of his priorities the development of a kegging plant. David was appointed a Director in 1966, and Frederic retired in 1969 due to ill health.

Frederic Robinson M.Sc. Tech., B.Sc., F.R.I.C. 1891-1969.

IN THE late 1960's the brewing industry went through a merger phase, with the number of breweries decreasing to 220 by 1968, although total beer production actually increased towards the end of the decade. For Stockport, now with an engineering base after the decline of the silk, cotton and hat-making industries, the 1960's were relatively prosperous. The town became a regional shopping centre and turnover grew more rapidly than any other major centre in the Manchester area. Robinson's, with a secure home base and a wide-ranging licensed estate, were able to

It was pints all round!

Mr Robinson (centre) performing the ceremony as the builders toast the accasion. TS 2116

THE new bottling and ware-housing centre for Frederic Robinson Ltd, the Stockport-based brewery, moved a stage nearer to completion, last week with a "topping-out" ceremony on the site, in Ashton Road, Bredbury.

This was carried out by Mr W. Cecil Robinson, and among those present were other directors, together with representatives from Pochin, the builders, and the architects, the Mark Jennings Partnership, of Hertfordshire.

The new plant will come into operation later this year, and a brewery spokesman explained: "Until now our bottling and warehousing facilities have been carried out at two separate locations in Stockport. When this building is complete it will enable us to bottle all our products under one roof, with other proprietary brands."

"There is also sufficient space on this site to accommodate all our activities although at the moment we have no plans for moving," he added.

continue improving their production facilities; a kegging plant was added in 1965-6 and a new wort cooling plant was installed at the brewery in 1970.

ALTHOUGH THESE refinements of the brewery plant were important, more significant for the future development of the company was the construction of the new bottling plant at Ashton Road, Bredbury in 1973-75; it was one of the largest ventures ever undertaken by Robinson's. It had been clear since the late 1960s that the combined bottling facilities at the Unicorn Brewery and Hempshaw Brook Bottling Stores were becoming inadequate, and the land bought in 1919 with the Horsefield Arms at Bredbury was selected as the site for a new plant. In making this decision, it was recognised that the site was considered to be of sufficient size to enable all of the company's operations to be housed there at some future time, if this was considered desirable.

The land bought in 1919 with the Horsefield Arms (above) at Bredbury was selected as the site for a new bottling plant.

THE BREDBURY site, which covers 9.72 acres, had originally been suggested as part of the route for a new road, but despite this, outline planning permission was granted at the end of 1971 for the first phase of building. This included a bottling unit, designed for flexibility, with the capacity to deal with short runs of many different products, as well as a large stockroom. After two years of detailed planning, building work began on the 14th November 1973, and on the 2nd July 1974 the foundations were given their finishing touch by Sir John and his six grandchildren, when a time capsule was placed beneath the plaque which is now at the main entrance.

BUILDING TOOK just under two years and was not without its difficulties. The flow on the entire drainage system had to be reversed, while a roof shell for the bottling hall was dropped, fortunately without damage to workers or plant. Another incident involved a large and expensive hole, needed to deal with the

Mr Cecil Robinson, the first Company President.

Sir John with his sons' children at the stone laying ceremony at the start of building of the bottling plant – (left to right) Veronica, Juliet, Oliver, Rachel (held by Sir John), Paul and William.

drainage. Excavation cost £30,000, but the hole turned out to be unnecessary when mains drainage became available; the hole was eventually filled in. Finally, the first bottling took place on the 15th October 1975, with distribution from Bredbury commencing in the following week.

THE UNICORN Packaging Centre at Bredbury was officially declared open by the Rt. Hon. Viscount Boyd of Merton on the 21st October 1976. A large number of guests were present, who were entertained to lunch in a marquee, and were then given conducted tours of the plant and premises, where Light Ale was being bottled.

1976 WAS a significant year for Robinson's, as it marked the centenary of the purchase of the Railway Inn at Marple Bridge,

The Tank Room contains the latest computerised equipment with a further 11 multi-purpose tanks, each holding 250 barrels sited externally.

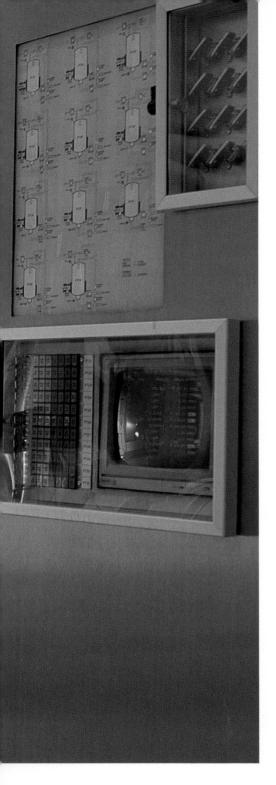

The plant cleaning centre provides computerised, automated cleaning of all mains beer tanks and road tankers.

All bottles pass through an empty bottle inspection machine before proceeding to the filler, which will fill bottles at the speed of 7,000 - 16,000 bottles per hour, depending on the size.

*Alan Machen, landlord of the Brown
Cow at Winton unveils a plaque at
the Unicorn Brewery in memory of
Sir John Robinson.*

Sir John Robinson.

*Dennis Robinson and Josephine
Slater married 22nd April 1967.*

and the start of the growth of the estate. Sadly Sir John, who had done so much to ensure the continued health and expansion of the company, died suddenly at his desk at the brewery on the 21st February 1978. He had been Chairman for forty-five years, and had overseen the acquisition of Bell's, the expansion of the licensed estate into North Wales and the construction of the new plant at Bredbury. One of his most important contributions to Robinson's came in the late 1930s, when under his Chairmanship the company pursued the policy of buying country pubs. Sir John and his brothers saw even then that the future lay with catering for the family and not just the urban drinker.

Sɪʀ Jᴏʜɴ was educated at Stockport Grammar School, and showed a keen interest in the brewery business from boyhood, often accompanying his father, William Robinson, on visits to pubs in the Robinson estate. He took a law degree at Manchester University, qualifying as a solicitor in 1918, and joined the family firm in the same year. He saw enormous changes in his sixty years with the company, and his efforts did much to help ensure its continued success.

Aꜰᴛᴇʀ ᴛʜᴇ death of Sir John, Cecil relinquished his joint Managing Directorship and became Company President, a new post for Robinson's. Peter took over the Chairmanship, making the fifth generation of Robinsons wholly responsible for the affairs of the company. Under the new Chairman, the company pursued its programme of pub refurbishment, which required a large investment, and continued to modernise the production plant; two new fermenting vessels were installed in 1978-9. By the end of the 1970s the brewing trade had been reduced to only 142 breweries owned by eighty-one companies, with the six major companies accounting for over three-quarters of the total production. Given this situation, combined with the revived interest in real ale, further investment

Peter Robinson.

in the company's plant was necessary to meet the challenges of the 1980s.

In the Robinson family, the 1960s saw the marriage of all three brothers of the fifth generation: Peter in 1963 to Barbara West, Dennis in 1967 to Josephine Slater and David in 1968 to Anne Preston. The first of Sir John's grandchildren, Dennis and Josephine's daughter Veronica, arrived in July 1969, followed a month later by David and Anne's son Paul. There are now nine members of the sixth generation of Robinsons, while the last of the fourth generation, Company President Cecil, died in 1980.

David Robinson and Anne Preston married 8th June 1968.

The Robinson family together at the opening of the Fletchers Arms, Denton, July 1986.

Peter Robinson and Barbara West married 28th Sept 1963.

EXPANSION ON the home front, at both the Unicorn Brewery and the Unicorn Packaging Centre at Bredbury, in the 1970s was followed in 1982 by the first Robinson brewery acquisition for over thirty years, that of Hartleys (Ulverston) Limited, another family firm.

The Ship, Bowmanstead, situated close to the picturesque village of Coniston, and within easy reach of the famous lake pictured here which Donald Campbell used for his world speed record.

You can still see the famous Hartleys Cask Head lovingly displayed outside some Lakeland pubs.

INTO THE LAKES

Tʜᴇ ʜɪsᴛᴏʀʏ of Hartleys can be traced back to the middle of the eighteenth century, when the town of Ulverston was the home of two breweries, the Old Brewery and Gill Brewery. The Old Brewery was built in 1755 by John Booth and James Machell, while the Gill Brewery had been in existence since at least 1751, when it was owned by the Clore family. Mid-eighteenth century Ulverston was a small but growing market town in Furness, that part of the Lake Counties within 'Lancashire North of the Sands'. It later became a textile and ironmaking centre, but although a canal was built in 1797 to join the town to the Leven Estuary and Morecambe Bay, it was a failure as a port.

The Old Brewery, Ulverston

"Here's another fine Pub you've gotten me into!"

Stan Laurel was born just a stone's throw away from the Old Brewery, Ulverston.

Tʜᴇ ɢʀᴏᴡɪɴɢ tourist trade was an important factor behind the increase of coaching traffic during the second half of the eighteenth century, and inns throughout the Lake District benefited. Ulverston's Sun Inn was one of the more notable inns of the time. Ulverston's two breweries continued in production, although ownership of the Gill Brewery passed through the hands of a succession of owners, Jackson, Benson then Askew, before it was bought by the Yarker family in 1800. It was sold again, to the Robinson family (no relation to Frederic Robinson) in 1834. As the population grew, housing conditions in mid-nineteenth century Ulverston worsened, although during the 1890s industrial workers from nearby Barrow moved to Ulverston, as Barrow could provide no accommodation. The combination of industrial workers and tourists provided a good trade for the Furness breweries.

Left, the Old Brewery Bottling Department, below a John Booth cheque, pre 1896.

IN 1892, in the the area overseen by the licensing justices of Barrow-in-Furness, there were ninety-five licensed houses to serve this mixed industrial and rural population. Over half were individually owned, sometimes by the landlord, but there were six firms with more substantial holdings, including the Furness Railway Company with its railway hotels. Burton companies Ind Coope and Burton & Lincoln Breweries owned five and seven houses respectively, James Thompson of Barrow owned six houses and Case & Co, also of Barrrow, seven. James Thompson & Co Ltd was an unusual firm, in that it never possessed its own brewery. Before 1932 Thompson brewed at another Barrow brewery, Heath's, and also at Chorley in Lancashire, but from 1932 they used Hartley's Old Brewery. Their brews were completely separate from Hartleys and supervised by Thompson's own brewer.

IT WAS the 17th July 1896 before the firm of Hartleys came into existence, when Robert and Peter Hartley of Burnley bought the Old Brewery and its eleven fully licensed houses (one on lease), fourteen beerhouses and thirty-one cottages. The Old Brewery

had been successful, with 1895 profits of £3,285 and steadily increasing trade. Its output at the time of purchase was 4,001 barrels per year and 1,380 dozen bottles, all bottled at the brewery. There was also a store for the wine and spirits trade, with an annual turnover of £900. The brewery itself covered 400 square yards and had its own ninety foot borehole producing fresh Cumbrian spring water. A stout and three types of Pale Ale, from XXX to X were brewed, the most expensive being the stout at £2 8s a barrel.

Above, and main picture, a camera faithfully records life at the Old Brewery in 1871.

SHORTLY AFTER their purchase of the Old Brewery, the Hartley brothers bought the Gill Brewery from its Leeds-based owners. In early September 1896, the two breweries became fully

Stockport brewers take over at Hartleys

CONTROL of Hartleys, the Ulverston real ale brewers, passed from one family to another this week.

The formal take-over of the brewery by Stockport based Robinsons was accepted by Hartleys shareholders on Monday.

Robinsons, real ale brewers themselves, now hold 80 per cent of the Ulverston company's shares.

But Hartleys fans and the brewery workforce have been told they need have no fears.

The brewery, its beer, its pubs and the Hartleys name are to remain. Mr Tim Hartley who remains company chairman told the Gazette on Monday: "I don't think members of the public will notice any difference."

"Written into the contract is the undertaking that brewing will continue for the foreseeable future and certainly for at least five years.

"Except with my consent there will be no compulsory redundancy of any of Hartley's present employees within five years."

Mr Hartley, who remains on the board with managing director Mr Tony Wallis, said the seven Hartleys directors had been unanimous in their decision to recommend the offer from Robinsons to shareholders.

But it means resignations for Mr Hartley's father, Col E. R. Hartley, former chairman of the board, and directors Mr Eric Simpson, Mr Hart Jackson, Mr Bob Darling and Mr Michael Bates.

Mr Hartley said: "In this day and age small breweries the size of ours need to join up with larger organisations to cut their costs, be able to buy materials and stock at a bigger discount and meet the challenge of national competition."

Taxation placed a small family-owned business at risk, he said, should estate or death duties suddenly become payable. The brewery might have had to be sold in a hurry not necessarily to the best buyer and against the interests of the product and the labour force.

Mr Hartley said Robinsons had "a great reputation for their real ale" and he said there should be no fears about the Ulverston brewery producing beer worthy of the name of Hartleys for many years come.

Robinsons chairman, Peter Robinson, who co onto the Hartleys Board his brothers Dennis and Da said Monday was probably most important day in history of both families.

He said the Hartleys would continue along wit beer and its pubs. "Hartleys a very great reputation fo traditional draught beer, said. "I hope that perhaps some time it will be possi have some Robinsons be Hartleys houses and Robinsons pubs will take of Hartleys beer."

Hartley's Ulverston brewery.

Eric's cottage industry

IT'S not often that the managing director of a brewery stops a press interview in its tracks, leads you out through the loading bay, across the road to his idyllic cottage and into the front parlour where he switches on the electric organ and plays you the hymn he wrote when his wife died.

Nor are there many who give pride of place in their office to a crumpled piece of the boat in which Donald Campbell crashed while attempting the world water speed record on nearby Coniston Water.

Or refuses to allow a beer sampling room on the premises, preferring to send over the road to the pub for beer whenever visitors arrive.

It is the measure of Eric Simpson, who is retiring at the end of the year as managing director and head brewer of Hartleys at Ulverston, that all these eccentricities appear entirely natural parts of his jovial and convivial character.

Eric Simpson went to Hartleys direct from Ulverston Grammar School after his headmaster, despairing of his academic career, sent him for an interview. He has been there ever since — 45 years in all — working his way from chief cask and bottle washer to managing director.

He unashamedly takes most of the credit for the changes which, in the past 20 years, have taken Hartleys from an ailing local brewery selling 70 barrels of beer a week to a lauded county concern averaging 400 barrels.

He has no connections with the ruling families of Hartleys brewery: the Robinson Hartleys and Darlings who began brewing in 1754 and have run the brewery ever since. But his presence has entirely eclipsed them.

When he took over the reigns he introduced a new best bitter called XB. In the first few years it sold just ten barrels a fortnight, he says, but now its his biggest seller.

It has attracted so much attention that for a while it was sold at the CAMRA Investments pub in faraway Greater Manchester.

Havoc

Eric Simpson is a man who gives himself entirely to his job. In his cottage over the road from the brewery he spends his evenings constructing elaborate multi-coloured graphs of his company's achievements.

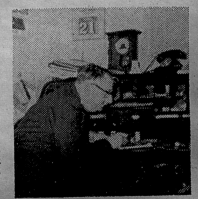

The display of 20-years sales figures hung in his office looks like a graph of 19th century population growth. Only in the last three years, as heat waves played havoc with uncooled pub cellars, have sales shown any signs of faltering.

Col. E. Robinson Hartley, appointed to the Board of Directors 1953, Chairman of the Board 1954, resigned as Chairman 1979 and appointed President. Resigned as President and Director 1982.

Cuttings from the Westmorland Gazette – top, announcing Robinson's take-over and below, in praise of Eric Simpson, Head Brewer 1957, Joint Managing Director 1964, Managing Director 1977, Vice Chairman 1978 until retirement.

Photographs from Eric Simpson's album – anticlockwise from top, Bobby Cloudsdale washing casks. Billy Moore cutting Billy Preston's hair. George Preston, Larry Tyson, J. Pattinson, Billy Preston on a Brewery Trip, 1920.

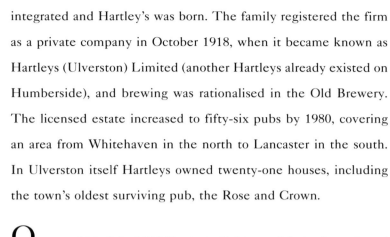

integrated and Hartley's was born. The family registered the firm as a private company in October 1918, when it became known as Hartleys (Ulverston) Limited (another Hartleys already existed on Humberside), and brewing was rationalised in the Old Brewery. The licensed estate increased to fifty-six pubs by 1980, covering an area from Whitehaven in the north to Lancaster in the south. In Ulverston itself Hartleys owned twenty-one houses, including the town's oldest surviving pub, the Rose and Crown.

On the 26th July 1982 Frederic Robinson Limited purchased Hartleys, adding its fifty-six houses to the existing Robinsons estate of 360 houses and off-licenses in north-west England and North Wales. The Hartleys estate with its many country pubs fitted in well with the Robinsons estate, and the two breweries, both family firms, had similar draught beer brewing traditions. The Old Brewery continued to brew "Beers from the wood" as well as the new ale Fellrunners, introduced in 1988.

The acquisition agreement had guaranteed that brewing would take place at Ulverston for five years, and indeed it continued well beyond that time. However, on the 7th June 1991 it was announced that brewing would cease at the Old Brewery later in the year. The last brew was mashed on the 21st October 1991, and the brewery closed on the 8th November. This was a sad event, and the decision to cease brewing was not taken lightly. Regrettably, the volume of beer brewed at Ulverston had been falling for some time, partly as a result of increasing sales of Robinson's own brands in Cumbria. As a result of the closure there were eight redundancies at the Old Brewery, but the premises are still actively used as a distribution depot serving Hartleys houses and free trade customers, as well as being the administrative base for the Hartley estate. The Hartleys presence in Ulverston will be secured by the future development of the site.

AN INDEPENDENT FUTURE

EXPANSION AT Robinson's continued during the 1980s initially with the transfer of kegging operations from the brewery to the second phase of building at the Unicorn Packaging Centre, Bredbury in 1980. The highly automated kegging line, commissioned in January 1981, originally functioned at a rate of thirty-five barrels per house, but now handles the kegging process, from washing to refilling, at an impressive seventy barrels per hour.

WHEN THE Unicorn Packaging Centre was first commissioned, the single refrigerated tank room contained twelve tanks, which totalled 800 barrels of capacity. This supplied a bottling line which handled three sizes of returnable bottles. Since 1975, further substantial investment in plant and buildings, all designed with an emphasis on modern technology and energy conservation, has increased the beer storage capacity to 4,350 barrels. High levels of quality control are standard throughout the Packaging Centre.

Opposite, from the left, David, Dennis and Peter Robinson (Chairman).

THE BOTTLING line is now able to handle a wide variety of the increasingly popular non-returnable bottles, as well as the traditional returnables. Contract bottling work proved to be a fruitful growth area in the early 1990s, with the contract volume increasing by a third over the year ending in May 1993, and coming to dominate the bottling volume. Changes in the brewing industry are quickly reflected in bottling, where novelty bottle shapes and sizes, small runs and fast turn-round times are now all part of the day's work.

As well as undertaking deliveries close to the brewery,
Robinson's Shires are a familiar sight at carnivals and shows over a wide area – often winning coveted awards.

Waggons used by Robinson's in the early Forties.

The Thorneycroft Waggon was a familiar pre-war sight, delivering ale to Kay's pubs in the North West.

IN THE late 1980s, while the third stage of development at the Bredbury complex took place, improvements kept the Unicorn Brewery competitive; updating of plant continued, with a new copper commissioned in the brewhouse during February 1986. The delivery fleet also expanded, to include a trunker and a tanker, but tradition was not forgotton; Robinsons still retain their award-winning team of two fine Shire horses, with restored exhibition drays and a 1927 Thorneycroft waggon. The Shires undertake deliveries near the brewery, and frequently participate in shows and carnivals.

Robinson's Hatters Mild. 'Hatters' is a name synonymous with Stockport for over 200 years, because of the town's famous hat-making industry, and is symbolised by the traditional bowler hats worn by Robinson's horsemen when showing their famous Shire horses.

A lovingly restored, 1927 Thorneycroft Waggon.

AFTER THE acquisition of Hartleys in 1982, Robinson's continued with plant renewal and pub refurbishment, spending a record sum on these items in 1985 as well as increasing the size of the Welsh estate. On the 14th July 1986, Lady Robinson opened the refurbished Fletcher's Arms in Denton, just north of Stockport, and an enjoyable ceremony was attended by three generations of Robinsons. Peter became Chairman of the North West Brewers Association in 1985, following in the footsteps of his father, Sir John, who was Chairman of the Manchester and District Brewers Association, one of the precursors of the North West Brewers' and Licensed Retailers' Association, as it is now known. Peter retired from the post of Chairman of the Association in the early 1990s.

THE ROBINSON's range of beers, included an award winner in 1987, when Robinsons Pale Ale won a Brewing Industry International Award. This was followed by a triumph for Robinsons Old Tom in 1990, when it carried off the strong ale category of the Campaign for Real Ale's Champion Beer awards. In addition, Robinsons Best Bitter became available in cans for the first time during 1987.

FREDERIC ROBINSON Limited entered the 1990s as the country's ninth largest regional brewer, owning 377 pubs and employing a workforce of over 450, including those in the managed houses and hotels. But for the brewing industry, the start of the 1990s was a difficult period, with another series of brewery mergers and closures, and the sale of many public houses. These activities were side-effects of the Monopolies and Mergers Commission report on "The Supply of Beer", published in March 1989. The company joined this hectic round of house sales and disposals in July 1991, buying fourteen Cumbrian pubs from

Pale Ale is a winner – first prize in its class at the Brewing Industry International Awards, 1987.

The Swan,
Little Urswick, Ulverston.

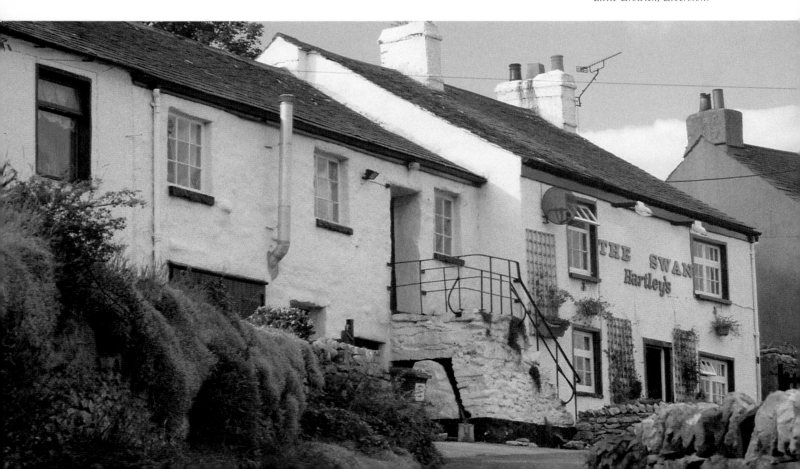

Paragon Inns, and followed this with the purchase of nineteen pubs from Bass between March and June 1992. The latter houses ranged from the Bird in Hand, at Ulverston, through the Woodtop and the Coach and Horses, both in Burnley, to the Masons Arms at Stockport.

THE COMPANY has survived and thrived as a family business, and is still led by Chairman Peter Robinson, whose main responsibility is the estate. Tragically, Peter's wife Barbara, who for many years designed and painted the company's inn signs, died in January 1991 after a long battle against cancer. Dennis Robinson oversees buying, marketing and wines and spirits, while David

Dennis Robinson (third from the right) on a visit to the Madeira Wine and Spirit association.

Best Bitter became available in cans for the first time in 1987.

Robinson is the production director. He and the Company's head brewer David Mercer, who retired in March 1994, had worked alongside each other for over thirty years, a period of dramatic change on the one hand, yet giving great stability to the philosophy of always putting quality first. All three brothers live in Cheshire and take a strong interest in local affairs. The strength of Robinson's bond with its home town is exemplified by company sponsorship of the local association football team, Stockport County, which began with the 1992-93 season.

ROBINSON'S IS the epitome of a traditional family brewery in an industry which can boast fewer and fewer of these once-common businesses. Indeed, in April 1993 the remaining breweries still under family control came together to form the Independent Family Brewers of Britain, an association which aims to promote the case for family brewers, tied houses and consumer choice. The Robinson Shire team took part in the parade of drays and vintage brewery vehicles through the City of London which helped to launch the association.

THE HISTORY of Robinson's now stretches back for well over two centuries. This is a substantial achievement with many important landmarks, beginning with the building of Ulverston's Old Brewery in 1755 and William Robinson's purchase of the Unicorn Inn in 1838. Then came the brewing of the first Robinson's around 1850, the registration of Frederic Robinson Limited in 1920, and the acquisition of local competitors Bell's in 1949. Nearer the present day, the opening of new facilities at the Unicorn Packaging Centre, Bredbury in 1975, and the acquisition of Hartleys in 1982 were two most significant events.

ROBINSON'S HAS managed to combine tradition and progression in a manner which holds continued appeal for its customers. All five generations of Robinson's involved in the firm have contributed to its record of good management, particularly during the 1890s and 1930s when other breweries were pursuing policies they later came to regret. With a sixth generation of Robinson's currently becoming part of the company, it seems certain, even given the harsh realities of the brewing industry in the late twentieth century, that Robinson's, currently involved in their largest ever investment on production that has ever been undertaken, will successfully continue into the next century and beyond. Cheers!

To celebrate Robinson's 150th Anniversary the Brewery produced a commemorative special ale which was universally well received.

THE ROBINSON FAMILY TREE

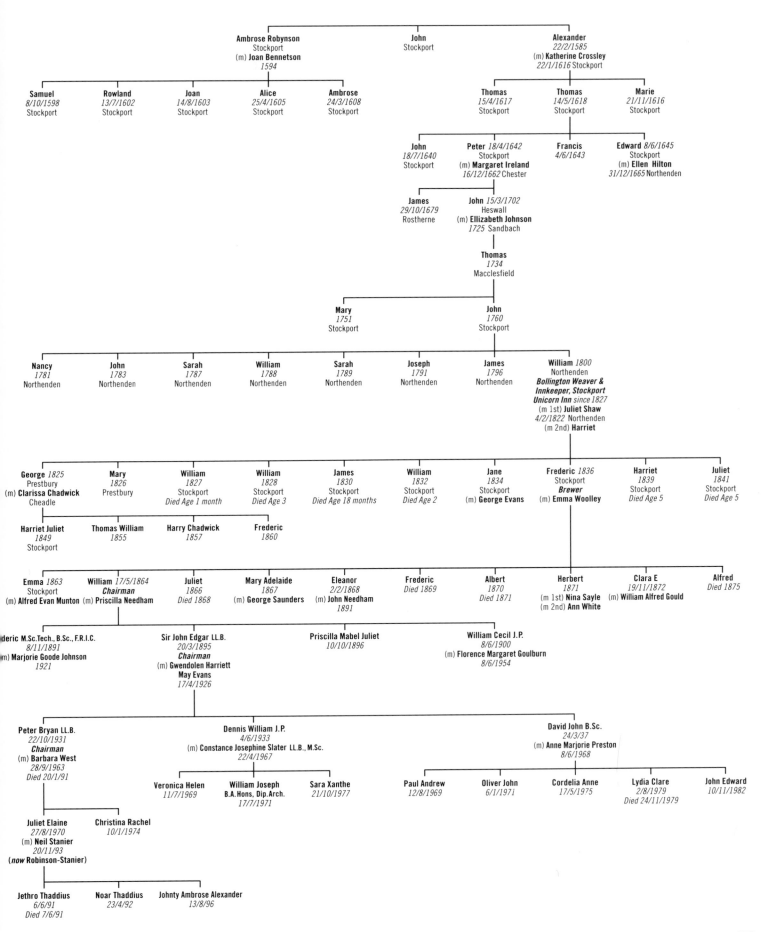

ALL OUR OWN WORK

When Chairman Peter Robinson met his wife Barbara she was an accomplished textile designer, a career she willingly gave up to care for her family.

Having only ever worked with water colours and, realising that this was a totally different art form, as she would be using oil based paints for the first time, Barbara offered to paint a sign for the Brewery. Peter agreed, and the first sign that Barbara re-painted was for the Royal Oak in Cheadle.

From then until the time of her death, Barbara was the artistic influence of the family business, designing and painting most of the signs outside Robinson's houses, and repainting the rest, including intricate coats of arms.

The first sign she designed was the Three Crowns; Hurdsfield. At the time Robinson's opened quite a number of new houses, and Barbara designed the signs for the March Hare; Ashton-under-Lyne, the Pied Piper at

Until the time of her death in 1991, Barbara Robinson (above) was the artistic influence of the family business, designing and repainting most of the signs outside Robinson's houses.

The first sign Barbara designed was the Three Crowns, Hurdsfield, followed by the March Hare, Ashton-under-Lyne, The Pied Piper at Little Hulton and The George and Dragon, Holmes Chapel.

Barbara was particularly pleased with this sign she painted for the Boar Hound in Macclesfield.

Little Hulton and the George and Dragon, Holmes Chapel.

In the beginning Barbara worked from home, moving briefly to a room over the cottage adjoining the Admiral Rodney in Prestbury, until alterations at home were completed and she had a fully equipped artist's studio over the garage.

As Barbara's health deteriorated her daughter Juliet assisted her mother by repainting some of the signs.

Juliet now designs and repaints all the signs for Robinson's houses.

Of the many signs that she designed, the one for the Tanronnen Inn at Beddgelert was Barbara's favourite, and indeed, it was much admired by the locals when it was first erected, as it depicts so much of the history of Beddgelert.

Not surprisingly, when the sign needed re-painting following recent major alterations, Juliet copied the original design to the letter, as a tribute to her mother.

Main picture – Juliet, continuing the family tradition initiated by her mother Barbara, now designs and repaints all the signs for Robinson's houses.

The Tanronnen Inn, Beddgelert was Barbara's favourite design. After major alterations to the Inn, Juliet repainted the original sign to the letter, as a tribute to her mother.

Each new sign is a challenge to Juliet's artistic skills.

THE BREWING PROCESS

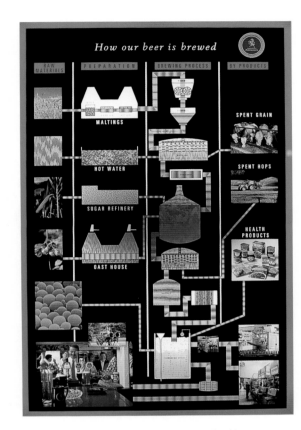

Visitors to the Brewery can study this illuminated diagram showing the flow of activities in the brewing process.

ONLY THE finest ingredients are used in our beers. Malt, which is made from barley; choicest hops which give the beers their distinctive bitterness and aroma; sugars and syrups. We have an excellent supply of first class water, specially drawn from deep bore holes at Unicorn Brewery.

The brewing process starts by grinding the malt. Hot water is added and the mixture is mashed; the resulting sugary liquid, or 'wort' is then separated from the husks.

The wort is transferred to large dome-shaped vessels called 'coppers' where it is boiled with the hops. The boiling process extracts the bittering resins from the hops, sterilises the wort and precipitates the residual protein. When the hops have been filtered off in the 'hop back' the wort will be bright and ready for cooling.

Following this the cooled wort is run into fermenting vessels where yeast is added. During the following four to seven days it feeds on the sugars and so produces alcohol. The yeast gradually turns the wort into beer. All this activity produces a thick, creamy layer of yeast on the surface of the brew which is skimmed off and the beer is transferred to casks. Traditional draught beer is 'living' in that some of the yeast remains in the beer when in cask.

The raw materials

Barley   *Malt*   *Crystal Malt*   *Roasted Barley*   *Hops*   *Sugar*

(Left) The yeast head is pulled back before dipping the vessel to ascertain the volume of liquid remaining.

This yeast feeds on the small amount of extra sugar added at this stage to produce a secondary fermentation and hence a natural sparkle to the beer. Finally, when the remaining yeast has settled the beer is ready to be served.

THE BREWING PROCESS

Malt is purchased from locations as diverse as Norfolk, Lincolnshire, Yorkshire and Scotland.

Sacks of malt are emptied into the malt hopper, in the background a 4-roller mill crushes the malt and removes dust and screenings.

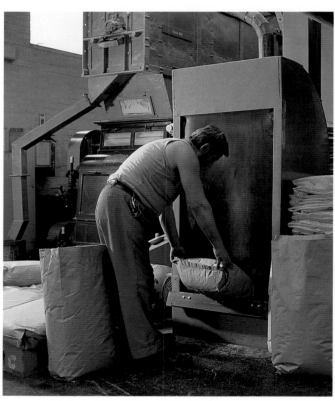

The mash is directed into the mash tun, where hot water is sprayed onto the mash or 'sparging' to wash through the extract.

Raw materials, the brewing process and the final product are monitored in the laboratory.

COPPER & S.D.V. No1

A sample of wort is taken from the copper to check for strength.

PRODUCTS

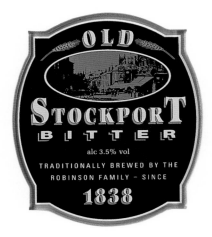

Hatters Mild
*Brewed with quality hops and barley
and cask conditioned to produce
a mellow, well balanced brew with
3.3% alcohol.*

Old Stockport Bitter
*Hoppy and refreshing, with 3.5%
alcohol, many customers prefer it as
a lighter alternative to Best Bitter,
especially at lunchtimes.*

XB
*Cask-conditioned in the time-honoured
manner XB is famed far and wide
for its rich body and is a smooth bitter ale
with a subtle tang of malt. 4% alcohol.*

BREWERY CONDITIONED

Cock Robin
*Specially brewed to provide the pleasures of Robinson's Bitter
where the demanding cellar conditions for cask-conditioned beers
are not available, it ensures consistent quality. 3.2% alcohol.*

Three Shires Mild
*Three Shires Mild with 3% alcohol, is a dark mild that is finding
favour beyond the three counties illustrated on the Font.*

Einhorn Lager
*A light straw colour and crisp refreshing character have made
this 4% alcohol lager very popular in Robinson's houses.*

Fellrunners Gold
*The well rounded flavour of this refreshing bitter, with 4.0% alcohol,
goes down well after a day out and about in the open air.*

Best Bitter

Its full, spicy bitterness from choice aroma hops, bright colour and lively head have made it Robinson's best-seller and one of the North-West's favourite pints. 4.2% alcohol.

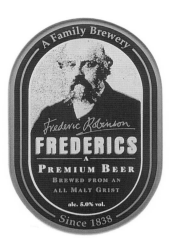

Frederics Premium Beer

Frederics is brewed from an all-British malt grist and only the finest, traditional aroma hop varieties. Containing 5% alcohol and packed with flavour, it has the immediate stamp of a quality beer.

Old Tom

A famous winter warmer and that rarity, an 'old ale' on draught, it has been brewed continuously since 1899 to produce a flavour richly redolent of the malted barley, 'winey' colour and no less than 8.5% alcohol.

Best Bitter
Also available in cans.

B O T T L E D

Old Tom
As well as being available on draught, Old Tom is also available in bottles.

Brown Ale
A deliciously dark ale with a sweet, creamy taste and 3% alcohol.

Shandy
The lemonade to bring out the best in the bitter is also made by Robinson's to their own recipe ensuring the distinctive flavour of this popular refresher.

Frederics
Also available in 275 ml and 500 ml bottles.

133

The Railway (*Royal Scot*) *Marple Bridge*	1876

HOUSES PURCHASED 1880s

Church Inn *Cheadle Hulme*	1880
Oddfellows Arms (*now Silver Jubilee*) *Heaton Norris*	1881
Bush Inn *Hyde*	1882
Gardeners Arms *Baguley*	1882
Church Inn *Edgeley*	1886
Nicholsons Arms Inn *Lancashire Hill, Stockport*	1886
Kings Arms *Fulshaw Cross, Wilmslow*	1887
Dandy Cock Inn *Disley*	1888

HOUSES PURCHASED 1890s

Arden Arms *Stockport*	1890
Royal Oak *Cheadle*	1891
Cow & Calf *Romiley*	1894
The Greyhound *Bredbury*	1895
The Bridge *Heaton Norris*	1896
The Fox *Brookbottom, Strines*	1898
Royal Oak *Stockport*	1899
Horse Shoe *High Lane*	1899
The Railway *Romiley*	1899
George & Dragon *Charlesworth*	1899
Northumberland Arms *Marple Bridge*	1899
The Railway *Handforth*	1899
The Bridge *Stockport*	1899

HOUSES PURCHASED 1900s

The Railway *Hale*	1900
Devonshire Arms *Ashwood Dale*	1902
George & Dragon (*rebuilt 1970*) *Holmes Chapel*	1904
Lowes Arms *Woodley*	1905
Royal Mortar *Stockport*	1905
Spread Eagle *Stockport*	1905

HOUSES PURCHASED 1910s

The Waggon & Horses *Matley*	1910
Tatton Arms *Wythenshawe*	1912
The Crown *Heaton Mersey*	1912
The Midland *Peak Dale*	1912
The Board Inn *Whaley Bridge*	1913
New Inn *Dukinfield*	1913
Honeywell Arms *Hathershaw*	1914
Coach & Horses *West Gorton*	1914
Bulls Head *Stockport*	1917
Queens Arms *Cheadle*	1917
The White Horse *Eccles*	1917
The Junction *Mottram-in-Longdendale*	1919
The Hunters *Chisworth*	1919
Horsefield Arms *Bredbury*	1919

HOUSES PURCHASED 1920s

Holly Bush *Bollington*	1920
Fletchers Arms *Denton*	1920
The Crispin *Great Longstone*	1920
Chapmans Arms (*rebuilt 1969*) *Hattersley*	1920
The Bluebell *Shaw, Oldham*	1920
Bulls Head *Castleton*	1920
New Inn *Buxton*	1920
The Manners *Bakewell*	1920
Rising Moon *Matley*	1920
Surrey Arms *Glossop*	1920
Hatters Arms *Marple*	1920
The Cock *Henbury*	1920
The Palatine *Hadfield*	1920
The Oxford *Werneth, Oldham*	1920
Prince of Orange *Ashton-under-Lyne*	1921
Red Lion *Lower Withington*	1921
Davenport Arms *Woodford*	1922
Red Bull *Church Lawton*	1922
The Queens *Werneth, Oldham*	1922
The Royal Oak *Oldham*	1922
Shoulder of Mutton *Chapel-en-le-Frith*	1923
Egerton Arms *Astbury*	1923
Grey Horse *Oldham*	1923
The Castle *Newton, Hyde*	1924
Swan with Two Necks *Stockport*	1924
Waggon Inn *Uppermill*	1925
Horse Shoe *Astbury*	1925
Old Hunters Tavern *Stalybridge*	1926
Arden Arms *Bredbury*	1927
Coach & Horses *Buglawton*	1927
The Pineapple *New Mills*	1927
Church House *Buglawton*	1929

SCHOLFIELDS HOUSES PURCHASED 1926

The Albion *Ashton-under-Lyne*
The Albion *Dukinfield*
Buck & Hawthorn *Ashton-under-Lyne*
The Caledonia *Ashton-under-Lyne*
Dysarts Arms *Micklehurst, Mossley*
Friendship Inn *Ashton-under-Lyne*
Friendship Inn *Glossop*
Gardeners Arms *Oldham*
The George *Hyde*
Highland Laddie *Mossley*
The Junction *Hazelhurst, Ashton-under-Lyne*
The Junction *Ashton-under-Lyne*
The Junction *Newton, Hyde*
Old Pack Horse *Audenshaw*
The Pineapple *Stalybridge*
The Snipe *Audenshaw*
The Tollemache Arms *Mossley*

KAYS ATLAS BREWERY HOUSES PURCHASED 1929

Bakers Vaults *Stockport*
The Bankfield *Hyde*
Black Horse *Preston*
The Castle *Manchester*
Church Inn *Failsworth*
The Florist *Stockport*

Foresters Arms *Higher Openshaw*
Hawk Inn *Haslington, Crewe*
The Junction *Oldham*
The Milan *Manchester*
New Inn *Hattersley, Hyde*
Pleasant Inn *Higher Blackley*
The Railway *Sale*
Royal Oak *Werneth, Oldham*
Star Inn *Higher Broughton, Salford*
Swan & Chequers *Sandbach*
Three Legs of Man *Greengate, Salford*
The Union *Reddish*
The Wheatsheaf *Whitefield*
White Lion *Hyde*
White Lion *Swinton*
White Swan *Fallowfield*
White Swan *Oldham*

HOUSES PURCHASED 1930s

The Healey *Rochdale*		1930
Cat & Fiddle *Wildboarclough*		1931
Waggon & Horses *Eaton*		1931
Flower Pot *Macclesfield*		1931
Legs of Man *Smallwood*		1932
Harrington Arms *Gawsworth*		1932
The Woodman *Hazel Grove*		1935
Bulls Head *Ashford in the Water*		1935
Bleeding Wolf *Scholars Green, Kidsgrove*		1935
Lawton Arms *Church Lawton*		1935
The Plough *Northwich*		1935
White Lion *Great Longstone*		1936
The Myersclough *Balderstone*		1936
The Broadoak *Ashton-under-Lyne*		1936
The Plough *Gorton*		1937
Grove Hotel *Buxton*		1937
Royal Oak *Mellor*		1938
Ye olde Admiral Rodney *Prestbury*		1939
Legh Arms *Prestbury*		1939

HOUSES PURCHASED 1940s

Shrewsbury Arms *Little Budworth*		1940
Red Lion *Little Budworth*		1941
Black Lion Hotel *Abergele*		1943
The Sycamore *Ashton-under-Lyne*		1943
Royal Ship Hotel *Dolgellau*		1944
Horse Shoe *Willaston, Nantwich*		1944
Bridge End Hotel *Llangollen*		1944
Bull I'Th'Thorn *Hurdlow*		1945
Saracens Head Hotel *Denbigh*		1945
Alvanley Arms *Tarporley*		1945
Prince Llewellyn *Beddgelert*		1945
Wynnstay Arms *Ruabon*		1945
Royal Oak *Garstang*		1946
North Western *New Mills*		1946
The Railway *Whaley Bridge*		1946
Rock Tavern *New Mills*		1946

Sandringham Hotel *Rhyl*	1946
The Waterloo *Taddington*	1947
Verdin Arms *Wimboldsley*	1947
Rising Sun *Tarporley*	1947
Ye Olde Cheshire Cheese *Longnor*	1947
Running Pump *Catforth*	1947
Griffin Hotel *Llanbedr-Dyffryn-Ruthin*	1948
The Smoker *Plumley*	1948

BELL & CO HOUSES PURCHASED JUNE 1949

The Armoury *Stockport*
The Adswood *Stockport*
Airport Hotel *Wythenshawe*
The Albion *Sutton, Macclesfield*
The Alexandra *Edgeley*
The Anchor *Hazel Grove*
Andrew Arms *Compstall*
Astley Arms *Dukinfield*
The Bay Horse *Newton*
Bird in Hand *Hazel Grove*
Blossoms *Heaviley*
Boars Head *Middlewich*
The Boarhound *Macclesfield*
The Brinnington *Portwood*
British Flag *Macclesfield*
Bulls Head *Kerridge*
Bulls Head *Marple*
Chapel House *Denton*
The Cock *Hazel Grove*
The Cock *Whaley Bridge*
The Crescent *Disley*
The Crossings *Furness Vale*
The Crown *Great Moor*
The Crown *Crewe*
The Crown *Hawk Green*
The Crown *Sandbach*
The Crown *Hyde*
Crown & Mitre *Chinley*
Dane Bank *Denton*
Devonshire Arms *Mellor*
Dog & Partridge *Bollington*
Dog & Partridge *Denton*
Dog & Partridge *Great Moor*
Dolphin *Macclesfield*
Duke of York *Heaviley*
The Emigration *Stockport*
Farmers Arms *Poynton*
Finger Post *Offerton*
Flying Dutchman *Stockport*
The Franklin *Macclesfield*
The Friendship *Romiley*
Gardeners Arms *Denton*
Gardeners Arms *Dukinfield*
George & Dragon *Macclesfield*
The George *Compstall*
The Grapes *Gee Cross*

The Grapes *Hazel Grove*
The Grapes *Edgeley*
The Grouse *Birch Vale*
The Grove *Hazel Grove*
Hare & Hounds *New Mills*
Hare & Hounds *Ludworth*
Horse Shoe *Crewe*
Iron Grey *Sandbach*
Jolly Carter *Chapel-en-le-Frith*
Kings William *Wilmslow*
Lord Byron *Macclesfield*
Manchester Arms *Stockport*
Market Tavern *Sandbach*
Masons Arms *Denton*
Masons Arms *New Mills*
The Midland *Elworth*
Moss Rose *Alderley Edge*
Nags Head *Macclesfield*
The Navigation *Marple*
The Navigation *Woodley*
New Inn *Chapel-en-le-Frith*
Oddfellows Arms *Hurst, Ashton-under-Lyne*
Old Pack Horse *Chapel-en-le-Frith*
The Organ *Hollingworth*
Park Tavern *Macclesfield*
The Pineapple *Marple*
The Pineapple *Stockport*
Printers Arms *Thornsett*
Printers Arms *Cheadle*
Queens Arms *Bollington*
Queens Arms *New Mills*
The Queens *Portwood*
The Railway *Rose Hill, Marple*
Red Bull *Stockport*
Red Cow *Nantwich*
Red Lion *High Lane*
Red Lion *Macclesfield*
Red Lion *Cheadle*
The Rifleman *Nantwich*
Ring O'Bells *Marple*
Robin Hood *Hazel Grove*
Royal Oak *Hazel Grove*
Royal Oak *Strines*
Royal Oak *New Mills*
The Sandpiper *Sandbach*
Sportsmans Rest *Bredbury*
Star & Garter *Stockport*
The Swan *New Mills*
Sydney Arms *Crewe*
Three Crowns *Hurdsfield*
Three Tuns *Hazel Grove*
The Tiviot *Stockport*
Travellers Call *Marple Bridge*
Travellers Call *Great Moor*
Travellers Rest *Sutton*

The Unity *Hyde*
The Unity *Stockport*
The Victoria *Dukinfield*
Vine Tavern *Birch Vale*
The Waggon *Mottram in Longdendale*
The Waterloo *Stockport*
The Wheatsheaf *Doveholes*
The White Hart *Hazel Grove*
The White Hart *New Mills*
White Horse *Disley*
Windsor Castle *Marple Bridge*

HOUSES PURCHASED 1950s

Ye Olde Boot Inn *Whittington*		1950
Kinmel Arms *Moelfre Bay, Anglesey*		1953
Duke of York *Flagg*		1955
White Hart *Flowery Field, Hyde*		1955
Jack & Jill **(new house opened)** *Brinnington*		1957
Windmill *Tabley*		1958

HOUSES PURCHASED 1960s

Cheshire Cat **(new house opened)** *Brinnington*		1960
March Hare **(new house opened)** *Ashton-under-Lyne*		1960
Square & Compass *Darley Dale*		1961
Pied Piper **(new house opened)** *Little Hulton*		1961
Vine Vaults *Ruthin*		1961
Tanronnen Hotel *Beddgelert*		1963
The Victoria Hotel *Llanbedr*		1964
Wildboar *Wincle*		1966
The Unicorn **(new house opened)** *Congleton*		1967
Gazelle Hotel *Menai Bridge, Anglesey*		1967
Vaynol Arms *Nant Peris*		1967
Bulls Head *Hale Barns*		1967
Anchor Inn *Tideswell*		1967
Rose & Crown *Allgreave*		1968
Four Crosses *Menai Bridge, Anglesey*		1968
George & Dragon *Beaumaris, Anglesey*		1968
The Pilot Boat *Dulas, Anglesey*		1968
Trecastell Hotel *Bull Bay, Anglesey*		1968
The Goat *Garndolbenmaen*		1969
Wanted Inn *Sparrowpit*		1969

HOUSES PURCHASED 1970s

The Woodman **(new house opened)** *Macclesfield*		1970
Brown Cow **(new house opened)** *Winton, Eccles*		1970
The Marquis *Rhosbol, Anglesey*		1970
Bulkeley Arms *Menai Bridge, Anglesey*		1970
The Bull **(new house opened)** *Macclesfield*		1971
The Peacock **(new house opened)** *Stalybridge*		1971
St. Tudwals *Abersoch*		1973
Red Admiral **(new house opened)** *Hulme*		1973
Breeze Hill Hotel *Benllech Bay, Anglesey*		1974
Puss in Boots *Stockport*		1974
Ark Royal *Harpurhey*		1974
The Plough *Llandegla*		1979

HOUSES PURCHASED 1980s

Wilbraham Arms *(new house opened)* *Alsager*	1980
Pant-yr-Ardd *Tregarth, Bethesda*	1980
Dusty Miller *Wrenbury*	1981
Saracens Head Hotel *Beddgelert*	1982
Sportsmans *Caergeiliog, Anglesey*	1985
Foundry Vaults *Llangefni, Anglesey*	1985
Glyn y Weddw *Llanbedrog*	1986
Brondanw Arms *Penrhyndeudraeth*	1986
The Red Lion *Hyde*	1987
Tophams Again *Rochdale*	1987
Harrington Arms *Bosley*	1989
The Linley *(new house opened)* *Alsager*	1989

HOUSES PURCHASED 1990s

New Inn *Castleton*	1990
Bulls Head *Glossop*	1992
Coach & Horses *Burnley*	1992
Cock & Magpie *Whitworth*	1992
Elleston Arms *Pilling*	1992
Golden Cross *Preston*	1992
The Grapes *Bamford*	1992
Mason Arms *Southport*	1992
Old Bridge Inn *Barrowford*	1992
Park Inn *Leek*	1992
The Plough *Hanley*	1992
The Railway *Woodley*	1992
Royal Oak *Littleborough*	1992
The Sycamore *Ashbourne*	1992
The Wellington *Bacup*	1992
The Woodtop *Burnley*	1992
The Whitchaff *Rawtenstall*	1993
Three Bears *(new house opened)* *Hazel Grove*	1994
Brindleys Lock *(new house opened)* *Stoke on Trent*	1995

HARTLEYS (ULVERSTON) HOUSES PURCHASED JULY 1982

Mermaid Tavern *Workington*
The Albert *Bowness-on-Windermere*
The Anchor *Ulverston*
Blue Bell *Egremont*
The Britannia *Ulverston*
Canal Tavern *Ulverston*
The Castle *Millom*
Cattle Market *Ulverston*
Cavendish Arms *Dalton-in-Furness*
Cross Keys *Milnthorpe*
The Crown *Coniston*
The Crown *Grange-over-Sands*
The Crown *Barrow-in-Furness*
The Crown *Cleator Moor*
Derby Arms *Ulverston*
Farmers Arms *Baycliffe, Ulverston*
Farmers Arms *Stainton, Barrow-in-Furness*
General Burgoyne *Great Urswick, Ulverston*
The Globe *Queen Street, Ulverston*
Golden Ball *Dalton-in-Furness*
Golden Rule *Ambleside*
The Harbour Hotel *Barrow-in-Furness*
Hope & Anchor *Grange-over-Sands*

Hope & Anchor *Daltongate, Ulverston*
Kings Arms *Barrow-in-Furness*
Kings Arms *Ulverston*
Lowther Arms *Hensingham, Whitehaven*
Manor House *Oxen Park, Ulverston*
Miners Arms *Dalton-in-Furness*
Miners Arms *Swarthmoor, Ulverston*
New Hall *Bowness-in-Windermere*
New Inn *Marton, Ulverston*
New Inn *Carnforth*
Old Friends *Soutergate, Ulverston*
The Ormsgill *Barrow-in-Furness*
The Outgate *Ambleside*
Piel Castle *Market Street, Ulverston*
Pig & Whistle *Grange-over-Sands*
Prince of Wales *Dalton-in-Furness*
Queens Head *Ambleside*
Red Lion *Lowick, Ulverston*
Red Lion *Millom*
Red Lion *Swarthmoor, Ulverston*
Robin Hood *Barrow-in-Furness*
Rose & Crown *Grange*
Rose & Crown *King Street, Ulverston*
Royal Oak *Grange-over-Sands*
Sawyers Arms *Kendal*
The Ship *Coniston*
The Swan *Little Urswick, Ulverston*
Swan Hotel *Swan Street, Ulverston*
The Unicorn *Ambleside*
The Union *Union Street, Ulverston*
The Victoria *Barrow-in-Furness*
Waggon & Horses *Lancaster*
Welsh Arms *Whitehaven*
White Hart *Kendal*

PURCHASED SINCE ROBINSON'S ACQUIRED HARTLEYS

Lunesdale Arms *Tunstall*	1985
Coach House *Bentham*	1987
Cumberland Inn *West Silloth*	1991
Dukes Head *Workington*	1991
The Globe *Distington*	1991
The Haywain *Little Corby*	1991
The Kingfisher *Cockermouth*	1991
The Limekiln *Brigham*	1991
Lowther Arms *Sandwith*	1991
Mermaid Tavern *Workington*	1991
Queens Head *Distington*	1991
The Ship *Kirkby-in-Furness*	1991
The Ship *Millom*	1991
The Stump *Prospect*	1991
Three Tuns *Whitehaven*	1991
The Tourists *Nethertown*	1991
The Wellington *Great Orton*	1991
Bird in Hand *Ulverston*	1992
Ship Inn *Roose*	1992
Dominics *Barrow-in-Furness*	1992
White Lion *Barrow-in-Furness*	1992
Lifeboat Inn *Maryport*	1994